THE PRIMACY OF THE CHURCH OF ROME

MARGHERITA GUARDUCCI

THE PRIMACY OF THE CHURCH OF ROME

Documents, Reflections, Proofs

Translated by
Michael J. Miller, M. Phil, M.A. Theol.

IGNATIUS PRESS   SAN FRANCISCO

Title of the Italian original:
Il primato della Chiesa di Roma
Documenti, riflessioni, conferme
© 1991 Rusconi Libri, Milan

Art credit:
Saint Peter in Cathedra
Bronze sculpture by Arnolfo di Cambio (c. 1245–1302)
St. Peter's Basilica, Vatican State
Copyright Scala/Art Resource, New York

Photograph credit:
View of St. Peter's Square and Basilica
Copyright Timothy McCarthy/Art Resource, New York

Cover design by Roxanne Mei Lum

© 2003 Ignatius Press, San Francisco
All rights reserved
ISBN 0–89870–922–9
Library of Congress Control Number 2002113297
Printed in the United States of America ∞

To the revered memory
of Gaetano De Sanctis, the greatest historian
of the ancient world and defender of Christianity,
who firmly believed in the primacy of the
universal Church of Rome

CONTENTS

PREFACE

The primacy of the Church of Rome is a subject debated over the course of many centuries and still of interest today. Its promoters and opponents have conducted their campaigns and even now take sides to discuss it. They are not always inspired by an uncompromising respect for the truth or by rigorous logic; some have even exhibited a certain passion that, among supporters of the thesis, has sometimes degenerated into counterproductive apologetics.

The task that I have set for myself in writing these pages is not to examine the primacy of the Roman Church in the way that this has been done as a rule until now, that is, considered exclusively as a theological and juridical problem. I propose instead to gather, to coordinate, and to expound simply and clearly the principal pieces of evidence that various other disciplines, too, offer us with respect to the thesis. Not only Christian but also pagan literature, philology, ancient, medieval, and modern history, archaeology, epigraphy: all these research materials concur, if I am not mistaken, in presenting us with a picture of that enormous problem that is in certain respects new. It is a picture spanning long centuries, from the dawn of Christianity until our age, interwoven with multifarious events, which are sometimes reassuring, sometimes highly dramatic, but always important and suggestive.

Contributing to the vividness of the picture, then, are certain "primacies" of Christianity that the Church of Rome maintains even today with respect to other Churches. I wanted to introduce these "primacies"—for the first time, I think—into the problem of the primacy and to highlight their most notable characteristics.

I did not want to exclude from the big picture the development of Roman history before the advent of Christianity. An examination of this development, in fact, permits us to recognize several significant events that, as if obeying a mysterious design, seem to have prepared the city of Rome very gradually to become the center of the universal Church.

I dare to hope that my presentation, which is based exclusively on sure evidence and always attuned to a dutiful respect for the scientific method, can be a consolation to those who read these pages by strengthening the faith in their souls.

And now, before entering into the thick of the material, I would like to turn my thoughts to the friends who, either in the course of my research or during the correction of the printer's proofs, were generous with their advice and provided information or assistance. To all of them goes this renewed expression of my most fervent gratitude.

E. G.

THE SPIRITUAL PRIMACY OF THE CHURCH
OF ROME IN EARLY CHRISTIANITY

This primacy is manifested several times, between the end of the first and the middle of the third century, in documents of various kinds that are associated and illuminate each other.

1. ROME, THE ANCIENT DESTINATION
OF CHRISTIAN TRAVELERS

The primacy of the Church of Rome in the age of Christian antiquity was very soon demonstrated by the voyages to Rome, often long and tiresome journeys, that the representatives of various Churches undertook. What could possibly have drawn them to the banks of the Tiber and braced them to confront, sometimes, dangers and hardships, if not the Roman Church, whose prestige of renown and of a real, preeminent authority was recognized? And in fact, as it turns out, they also came to Rome to present their problems to the heads of the Roman Church, to ask for advice and assistance. But they also came (and this is very significant) simply to know firsthand the Church that everyone was talking about. Indeed, the time came when the trip to Rome, for the faithful of the Christian world, took on the importance of a ritual.

Founded by the apostles Peter and Paul, who had suffered martyrdom in Rome (Peter, at least, in A.D. 64) and had been buried there, the Roman Church very soon began to attract the faithful of the other Churches; but this appeal exerted by the famous Church is evident above all in the course of the second century, a century rich in historical events and intense spiritual activity. The fascination of the Church of Rome made itself felt with particular force then—during the second and also during the third century—in the East, where Christianity had been born and had deeper roots.

Let it be noted, furthermore, that not only the Christians whose faith was pure, but also some of those who had separated themselves from the authentic trunk of Christianity to follow various branches of heresy proved to be sensitive to the appeal of the Roman Church, and they too wanted to come and get to know her.

But let us focus our attention on a few voyages that had Rome as their destination.

A little after the middle of the second century, around the year 154, Polycarp, the holy bishop of Smyrna, who boasted of having known John the Evangelist personally and even of having been his student, braved the inconveniences of a voyage from Smyrna to Rome so as to be able to discuss face to face with Anicetus, the pope of Rome, the delicate question of the date on which Easter should be celebrated; a question upon which great importance was placed at that time and about which the Churches of Asia dissented from the Church of Rome.[1] The meeting between Polycarp and Anicetus did not settle the disputes, and Polycarp, although he had taken leave of Anicetus in a spirit of peace, had to set out again to travel back to Smyrna, where not long afterward (sometime in the year 156 or 157) he died heroically as a martyr, burned at the stake.

---

[1] Cf. Eusebius, *Historia ecclesiastica* 5, 24, 16.

During the reign of Marcus Aurelius (161–180) a voyage to Rome was made by another bishop of Asia Minor, Abercius. He traveled from Hierapolis, a city in far-off Phrygia Salutaris, for the set purpose of becoming acquainted with the renowned Roman Church. But I will have to speak at somewhat greater length about Abercius farther on.[2]

At the end of the reign of that same Marcus Aurelius, in A.D. 178, to be precise, a famous Christian personage came to Rome who also had his origins in Asia Minor but who was by that time stationed in Gaul, in Lyons. I speak of the famous Irenaeus.

Most likely born in the vicinity of Smyrna, he had as his first teacher the holy bishop Polycarp, of whom I have already spoken; then, while still a youth, he emigrated—it is not known for what reasons—to Lyons, in the far West, and there he eventually became a priest of the bishop Pothinus. In 177 the persecution of Marcus Aurelius broke out, and Pothinus, who was already advanced in age, and other fervent Christians of the city were arrested and subjected to cruel torments; they withstood the ultimate test of their faith and became the famous "Martyrs of Lyons". In addition to the pains of persecution, these holy men had to suffer the anxiety caused by the spread of the Montanist heresy and by the reaction that this provoked on the part of the Roman Church. It was fitting, then, that the representatives of the Church of Lyons should send to Rome the young and energetic Irenaeus to confer with Pope Eleutherius (175–189). The purpose of this diplomatic mission was to ask the pope charitably to show indulgence toward the Montanists, so as to safeguard as much as possible the unity of Christians.

[2] See below, pp. 34–40.

After returning to Lyons and becoming the successor of Bishop Pothinus, who died in the persecution (178), Irenaeus eagerly set about spreading Christianity through Gaul. But in a little while I shall have to return to him, as I will to Abercius.

Continuing meanwhile our list of significant voyages to Rome and proceeding to the third century, we cannot pass over in silence the voyage of Origen, the great thinker and master of the Alexandrian school. He came to Rome while Zephyrinus was pope (199–217), not to discuss a particular issue that he had at heart, as Polycarp and Irenaeus had done, but for the sole purpose of knowing firsthand the renowned Roman Church.[3]

Polycarp, Abercius, Irenaeus, and Origen only made simple trips to Rome. For others, however, it was a matter of long sojourns.

Such was the case of Justin [Martyr], the famous Christian writer who sought in the Greek philosophy of Plato the beginnings of Christianity. Born in Palestine of pagan parents and having become a Christian, probably at Ephesus, he decided to relocate to Rome, and there he opened a school, taught, and wrote, and he ended by suffering martyrdom, around the year 165, during the reign of Marcus Aurelius.

Similarly, another Doctor of the Church, Hegesippus, a Judaeo-Christian as well, went to Rome and spent several years there between A.D. 175 and 180. His scholarly work was especially aimed at opposing the truths of the Christian faith to the supposed secret traditions of the Gnostic sects, and in order to do that he devoted himself to studying in greater depth the genuine tradition that the apostles had handed down. According to Eusebius of Caesarea, the author of the *Ecclesiastical*

---

[3] Eusebius, *Historia* 5, 14, 10.

History that I shall cite many times, Hegesippus would have had the means of studying this tradition at first in the Church of Corinth, and then above all in the Church of Rome.[4] Certainly, his contacts with the Church of Rome, and with the important Christian personages and cultural leaders there, must have helped him with the ponderous tome of *Memoirs* that Hegesippus wrote after his return to Jerusalem.

Thus the Church of Rome, from that ancient period onward, attracted Christian people who were true believers, but as I have already mentioned, no less strong was the attraction that she exerted, if only indirectly, upon the leaders of heretical movements.

During the pontificate of Hyginus (136–140), as the reign of Adrian ended and that of Antoninus Pius began, Rome was host to Valentinus, the founder of the heretical sect of the Valentinians. Of Egyptian origin, Valentinus had at first been a genuine Christian; then he was attracted by the mirage of lofty Gnostic speculations. Arriving in Rome, he had there a large following of disciples, who usually gathered in the quiet of shady suburban villages.

Valentinus was then joined, in the second century and in the first half of the third century, by other heretical thinkers who came to Rome, drawn not only by the prestige of the imperial city, but also, in the final analysis, by the fame of the Church which had her seat in Rome: Marcion, a native of Sinope on the Black Sea (ca. 139), Theodotus of Byzantium (ca. 190), Noetus of Smyrna, accompanied by his disciples Epigonus and Cleonimus (ca. 180–200). A woman, too, Marcellina, an active promoter of the Gnostic heresy founded by the Egyptian Carpocrates, came to Rome during

---

[4] Ibid., 5, 8–21.

the pontificate of Anicetus (155–166) and probably took up residence there. Later I will have occasion to return to the zealous Marcellina as well.[5]

These voyages, these more or less lengthy stays in Rome by genuine Christians and also by heretics, coming from the most diverse regions, demonstrate in and of themselves that during the most ancient period the Church of Rome enjoyed a primacy among the others and that the others sensed her fascination and recognized her authority. This is confirmed, as will be seen, by the statements of thinkers, both Christian and non-Christian, and also by epigraphs, among which the famous inscription of Abercius is outstanding for its exceptional importance.

But what—we might ask—were the reasons for this undeniable preeminence?

2. THE REASONS FOR THE PRIMACY AND THE *POTENTIOR PRINCIPALITAS* OF IRENAEUS

Some modern scholars, since they cannot overlook the effective preeminence of the Church of Rome in early Christianity, have speculated that the principal if not the sole reason for it was the political importance of Rome. Because Rome was, in that era, the capital of the empire, it is obvious (they maintain) that the Roman Church should have primacy over the others.[6] But this explanation, which is a bit too simplistic, encounters various difficulties. Among others, there is, as we shall see, the one consisting of certain precious words from the epigraph of Abercius.

---

[5] See below, pp. 84ff.

[6] I cite, among other works, that of Oscar Cullmann, *Petrus, Apostel-Jünger-Märtyrer* [Peter: apostle, disciple, martyr], 2d ed. (Zürich-Stuttgart, 1960), p. 266.

The power of Rome, the capital of the empire, contributed, no doubt, to the authority of the Christian Church that had come and taken up residence within its walls. But it is only a contribution. There were other motives, not of a political, but of a spiritual character that seem to have led to this preeminence.

Making progress toward solving this problem requires, first of all, rereading certain famous lines written by the aforementioned Irenaeus, bishop of Lyons—statements over which scholars have spilled rivers of ink.[7]

The worrisome passage is included in the work that Irenaeus wrote in order to refute heresies. In Irenaeus' time, in the second century, the spread of heresies was a cause of grave anxiety for "orthodox" (right-believing) men. We have already seen how, between 177 and 178, during the persecution of Marcus Aurelius, Irenaeus himself had been sent from Lyons to Rome to discuss with Pope Eleutherius the question of the Montanists and to request, in Christian charity, the pontiff's indulgence toward them. It was to refute these heresies and to make sure that the faithful would not fall prey to them that this same Irenaeus dedicated his principal work, in which precisely we find the passage that I have cited. The work, composed between 175 and 189 and originally written in Greek, has been preserved for us partly in the original Greek, partly in a Latin translation, partly in an Armenian version. The passage concerning the primacy of the Church of Rome is included in the Latin translation.

The opinion of Irenaeus takes on great importance for us, not only because of the authority of the one who expresses it, but also because Irenaeus, a son of the East (he was educated, you will recall, at the school of Polycarp, bishop of

---

[7] Irenaeus, *Adversus haereses* 3, 1–2.

Smyrna), represents at the same time, as bishop of Lyons, Christianity in the West.

In the passage that I have cited, Irenaeus asks first of all how it is possible to recognize the genuine Christian tradition. Sharing the thought that was expressed at around the same era, as we have seen, by Hegesippus, a Palestinian, Irenaeus focuses his attention (logically enough) on the message handed on from Christ's apostles to every Church that they would found. To find out the genuine contents of this message, we need—he declares—to trace back the series of bishops who succeeded one another in each Church, until we reach the beginning of each series. Irenaeus knows these series quite well and can recall the names of all the individuals in them up to the moment when he is writing. Yet because—he notes—the undertaking would be too long, he prefers to limit his investigation exclusively to the Church of Rome, that is, to the one that is (and these are his words) "the greatest and the most important[8] and best-known of all, founded and organized by the two most glorious apostles, Peter and Paul". Note, with regard to the expression "most glorious" (in Latin *gloriosissimi*), that this adjective is attributed, as is only right, precisely to persons who have undergone martyrdom and thereby attained glory. After a reference to the faith of the Romans, which is known throughout the world, Irenaeus continues:[9] "For with this Church, because of her more powerful preeminence [*poten-*

[8] The adjective *antiquissima* should be interpreted, not as "the oldest", but rather as "the most important" (cf. M. Guarducci, in *Rivista di filologia e d'istruzione classica* 105 [1977]: 311ff.).

[9] For the sake of clarity, here is the original text of Irenaeus: "Ad hanc enim ecclesiam propter potentiorem principalitatem necesse est omnem convenire ecclesiam, hoc est eos qui sunt undique fideles, in qua semper ab his qui sunt undique conservata est ea quae est ab apostolis traditio."

tior principalitas], all Churches must agree, that is, the faithful who come from every part [of the world]; and it is in her that the tradition that was handed from the apostles has always been maintained by the faithful who come from every part." At this point Irenaeus inserts the list of the bishops of Rome known by him, a list that includes eleven names, from Linus, the first successor of Peter, to Eleutherius (175–189). With regard to this last pope, let it be noted that the time of his pontificate is what suggests to scholars the date for Irenaeus' work *Against Heresies*. Irenaeus goes on to affirm that, through this uninterrupted series of bishops, the message of the apostles came down to us, demonstrating that there is "one and the same life-giving faith that has been preserved in the Church from the apostles to this day and handed down in truth."

On this passage, as I said, Church historians and philologists have written quite a few pages. A little of that great quantity of ink was spilled by me as well in a scholarly essay published more than ten years ago, an essay that still seems valid to me and therefore not without application to what I am writing now.[10]

In the passage from Irenaeus the reference to the "more powerful preeminence" (*potentior principalitas*) of the Church of Rome is, naturally, the focal point.

What reasons form the basis for the *potentior principalitas*, which is, practically speaking, the primacy that Irenaeus acknowledges in the Church of Rome?

The reasons are, essentially, the following:

1.   that she is the greatest and the most important;
2.   that she is renowned worldwide;

[10] M. Guarducci, in *Rivista*, pp. 307–20.

3.   that she was founded and organized by (both) the
      apostles, Peter and Paul;
4.   that she enjoys throughout the world the reputa-
      tion of having a steadfast faith.

All this corresponds to the truth. The Roman Church was
undoubtedly, in those days, the largest, and she was universally recognized. Then too, she had had the exceptional privilege of being founded by the two apostles who, after bringing
to Rome the message of Christ, had suffered martyrdom there
and had been buried in tombs that were still visible and venerated. Moreover, as to the distinction of preserving the faith
as it is known throughout the world, Irenaeus does no more
than re-echo the statement written by Paul in his Epistle to
the Romans: "Your faith is proclaimed in all the world." [11]

For reasons such as these Irenaeus attributes to the Church
of Rome a "more powerful preeminence", that is, an authority superior to that of any other Church. But this acknowledgment, in his eyes, opens up a grandiose vista. Because
the Church of Rome surpasses all the others in authority, "it
is necessary" (*necesse est*) for all the other Churches to defer
to her. In short, Irenaeus sees the Church of Rome ideally as
the center of the universal Church. One confirmation of
this thought is the statement that only in the Church of Rome
is the apostolic tradition preserved "by the faithful who come
from every part". I believe that in my article, cited above, I
have demonstrated for the first time the meaning of these
words, which are not entirely clear. Irenaeus, in my opinion,
wanted to draw attention to the circumstance that the leaders of the Roman Church, who gradually had handed on the
genuine apostolic tradition, belonged to various parts of the

[11] Rom 1:8.

Christian world. And in fact, if we examine the series of the successors of Peter, which Irenaeus includes precisely at this point, we notice that those men came from the most diverse regions: out of twelve, only four were of Roman heritage; the other eight harked back to a wide variety of localities (Tuscia, Greece, and in particular Athens, Aquileia, Syria, Campania, Epirus). All of these places in the Christian world were important in the series of those who, down to the age of Eleutherius, had guided the Roman Church, just as the most varied localities, both near and far, were represented by the faithful who came streaming into the Church of Rome. In another passage of the same work, *Against Heresies*, Irenaeus had characterized the Church of Rome as the visible center of all the Churches, which with her formed "a single body, a single soul, a single heart".[12]

With the concept of the supremacy of the Church of Rome over all the others is intertwined that of the universality of the Roman Church. This in turn is rooted in the concept of the universality of imperial Rome, which was already widely held by the pagans.

After the foundation of the empire by Augustus, poets, historians, and apologists did not miss a single opportunity to express and confirm the exalted idea that Rome, the capital of the empire, was the common fatherland of all the people in the world. Very soon they even hit upon the eloquent word-play pairing *urbis* (the genitive of *urbs*, that is, Rome, "the city" par excellence) with *orbis* (the nominative and genitive of the word signifying "the world"). The identification of Rome with the world lasted a long time, not only in Rome but elsewhere, too. Just think of the famous verses that

---

[12] Cf. Eusebius, *Historia* I, 10, 2.

Claudius Rutilius Namatianus, a Gallic poet, addressed to Rome at the beginning of the fifth century:

> *fecisti patriam diversis gentibus unam ...*
> *urbem fecisti quod prius orbis erat.*

"Thou hast made a common fatherland for various peoples.... Thou hast made a city out of what was formerly the world." [13]

Of particular interest to us, then, is the fact that the concept of the universality of Rome was deeply rooted in the thinking of Asia Minor during the second century, specifically in the native land of Irenaeus. This is clearly demonstrated by certain passages from Aelius Aristides (for the record, the author of the famous *Encomium of Rome*), who lived in Smyrna, that is, in the former see of Irenaeus.

In the same age, and again in Asia Minor, a Christian voice is heard exalting the close and providential ties between the universal empire of Rome and the Church of Christ. This is the voice of Melito, bishop of Sardis. A little after A.D. 170, perhaps in 171 or 172, this bishop wrote to the emperor, Marcus Aurelius, an *Apology*, with the intention of having him abolish or at least mitigate several recent ordinances that were detrimental to the Christian community of Asia Minor. In this written work, the pious and gifted Melito manifested his deference toward the ruler and government of Rome and took advantage of the occasion, first, to express several thoughts that would not fail to ingratiate the philosopher-king. Meditating on his own *philosophia*, that is, on Christianity, he went so far as to observe that a singular parallel existed between Christianity and the empire. The

---

[13] Rutilius Namatianus, *De reditu suo* 1, 63, 66.

Christian religion, which had flourished under Augustus, became, in his judgment, a sort of "foster sister" of the empire founded by that great ruler and providentially accompanied the development of it, so that from Augustus onward the empire constantly increased in prosperity and glory.[14]

Analogous thoughts would then be manifested in another *Apology* that another bishop addressed to the same Marcus Aurelius at around the same period, and from Asia Minor, of all places: I mean Apollinarius, bishop of Hierapolis in Phrygia.[15]

Turning now to Irenaeus and to his famous and oft-debated passage about the *potentior principalitas* of the Church of Rome, we can state confidently that he held the Church of Rome to be preeminent among the other Churches of the Christian world and was furthermore convinced, as were Melito and probably Apollinarius, that it was universal: a universality providentially attuned to the universality of the empire, of which Rome was the capital.

3. CORROBORATION FOR THE OPINION OF IRENAEUS:
THE SPIRITUAL PRIMACY OF THE CHURCH OF ROME
IN OTHER DOCUMENTS, BETWEEN THE END
OF THE FIRST AND THE MIDDLE
OF THE THIRD CENTURY

1. The Epistle of Clement of Rome to the Corinthians

We are at Rome, around A.D. 96, that is, about thirty years after Peter and Paul had undergone martyrdom as victims of Nero's persecution. The Church established by the apostles

---

[14] Cf. Eusebius, *Historia* 4, 26, 5–11.
[15] Ibid. (where, however, not one word from the *Apologia* is quoted).

receives unsettling news from the Church of Corinth. Some young men of that community, rebelling against the older priests, have deposed them. In this state of affairs Clement, who leads the Church of Rome, takes the initiative of intervening and writing his famous letter to the Corinthians.[16]

Roman by birth, he was, according to tradition, the third successor of Peter. It is uncertain whether, in that era, one can speak of a true pope in the strict sense, the sole head of the Roman Church, or rather of a college of priests over whom presided a *primus inter pares*, a first among equals.[17] Be that as it may, he was certainly at that time the most authoritative personage of the Christian community in Rome. Consequently, later on he came to enjoy great esteem, both in Rome and elsewhere. It is certain that in the city of Corinth itself his letter was later read during the Sunday liturgy.[18]

Now in writing to the Church of Corinth, Clement proposes to restore within her the harmony that has been lost. As a salutary example for the Corinthians who are torn by dissension, he recalls the perfect discipline of the Roman legion and, like Melito of Sardis later on, shows deference toward the rulers of the empire, for whom he foretells every divine grace. Seeking then to determine the root causes of the evil that is troubling the Church of Corinth, Clement does not hesitate to attribute it to envy and jealousy, and in this regard he cites ancient and recent examples that make it clear what lamentable consequences envy and jealousy can lead to. As for the distant past, the Old Testament offers the eloquent examples of Cain and Abel, Esau and Jacob. As for more recent times—quite recent, from the perspective of the

---

[16] Clement, in *Patrologia Graeca*, 1, 217–21.

[17] Cf. M. Simonetti, in *Vetera Christianorum* 26 (1989): 115–36.

[18] See below, p. 31.

author of the *Epistle*—he avails himself of examples taken from the Neronian persecution of A.D. 64. According to Clement, it seems that precisely during this persecution envy and jealousy had had some influence within the Christian community in Rome. To all appearances these very sentiments were, in the final analysis, the cause of the deaths of the apostles Peter and Paul and of a host of the elect—men and women who in the hour of their extreme peril had gathered around those leaders and had been sustained by their spiritual authority. To Clement we owe also certain information concerning the cruel spectacles that took place on that occasion in the Circus of Nero in the Vatican and which had as their protagonists the heroic Christians who underwent martyrdom there, giving to Christ the supreme witness of faith. This information is precious to us and is confirmed not many years later by what Tacitus, the great historian of Rome, would write in his *Annales*.[19]

The epistle of Clement to the Corinthians would make a great and lasting impression on that Church. We know for a fact from the *Ecclesiastical History* of Eusebius that around A.D. 170 the aforesaid epistle was still being read in the Sunday liturgy, together with an epistle that the bishop of Rome Soter (166–175) later sent to Dionysius, bishop of Corinth.[20] Subsequently the epistle of Clement spread from Corinth to other places and became a regular part of the liturgy of other Churches.

In his famous epistle to the Corinthians Clement does not refer explicitly to the primacy of the Church of Rome, but his very initiative of addressing and admonishing the Church of Corinth in the guise of a peacemaker demonstrates that

---

[19] Tacitus, *Annales* 15, 44.
[20] Eusebius, *Historia* 4, 23, 11.

he strongly sensed the spiritual preeminence of his Church and therefore the responsibility of that Church, which Irenaeus would later call *potentior principalitas*, with respect to the other Christian communities. On the other hand, the voluntary acceptance of the words of Clement on the part of the Corinthians—voluntary to such an extent that they had the epistle from Rome introduced into the liturgy, where it remained for several decades—shows that the second-century Corinthians fully recognized the preeminent spiritual authority of the Church of Rome.

2. The letter of Ignatius, bishop of Antioch, to the Romans

Passing beyond the confines of the first century, we suddenly come across an explicit affirmation of the spiritual primacy of the Church of Rome. I mean that of Ignatius, bishop of Antioch in Syria.

The Church of Antioch, founded in her day by the same Peter, was led at the beginning of the second century by a man of the highest spiritual caliber, Ignatius, who perhaps had had the good fortune to know personally the apostles Peter and Paul. The other Churches of Syria were probably also under his authority. In A.D. 107, at the beginning of the reign of Trajan, Ignatius, fallen into disgrace because of his courageous profession of the Christian faith, was imprisoned, condemned to death, and sent off to Rome, where the lamentable execution would take place. The death sentence consisted in being thrown to the wild animals (*ad bestias*), in one of the horrible spectacles in which the crowds of that day delighted. The place of execution would be the great Flavian amphitheater (the Coliseum), which had been completed a few years before and opened for the entertainment of the public.

Once he had embarked on the ship that was to bring him to his death, Ignatius meditated on his imminent martyrdom and on the eternal reward that would result from it. This splendor of faith shone with marvelous clarity in the letters he wrote from Smyrna, taking advantage of the stopover made in that locality by the ship on which he was voyaging. Outstanding among the letters in its importance is the one that Ignatius wrote to the Romans, that is, to the faithful of that city in which he would soon give to Christ the supreme witness of his faith. The letter, naturally, was intended to precede his arrival in the *urbs*, the city. A few scholars have raised some doubt as to the authenticity of the text, but in the opinion of the majority such doubts seem—for valid reasons—unfounded.

Anyone who reads the epistle of Ignatius to the Romans cannot fail to note that the Church of Rome occupied a preeminent position in the mind of Ignatius as well. Right away, at the beginning of the letter, he declares that the Church of Rome "presides in the region of the Romans" (προκάθηται ἐν τόπῳ χωρίου Ῥωμαίων). The preposition ἐν shows that the verb "preside" should be understood in the absolute sense, and not only with respect to the territory in which Rome is located. In other words, we need to understand that, according to Ignatius, the Roman Church presided, that is to say, was preeminent with respect to the other Churches of the Christian world. Ignatius then goes on to salute the Church of Rome with fervent expressions of honor and admiration; in vain would we look for anything comparable in the salutations he addressed to the other Churches when writing the letters whose texts have come down to us. Here is the series of laudatory epithets that Ignatius bestows upon the Roman Church: "worthy of God, worthy of honor, worthy of being called blessed, worthy of praise, worthy of success, worthy of veneration, which presides at the *agape*, which bears the name of Christ, which bears the Father's name: Her do I salute in the name of Christ, the Son of the Father", and so on.

There have been many debates about the words, "which presides at the *agape*" (προκαθεμένη τῆς ἀγάπης).

The Greek noun ἀγάπη means, in common usage, "love, charity". Ignatius, too, assigns this meaning to it more than once. Accepting this more common interpretation, some scholars have translated the expression in question with the phrase, "which holds the primacy in charity", which would be corroborated by the reputation for charitable activities that the Roman Church in fact enjoyed. But this interpretation, if I am not mistaken, runs into a difficulty. If Ignatius had wanted to express this thought, he would have used the dative τῇ ἀγάπῃ and not the genitive τῆς ἀγάπης. Besides the common meaning of "love, charity", the term ἀγάπη can also take on the meaning of a "banquet attended by men united with one another by a bond of love". Speaking in Christian terms, the word ἀγάπη can therefore be taken in the sense of "eucharistic banquet". There is yet another meaning that the word can have, and this is found, as it seems, only in the writings of Ignatius. This is the meaning "Church", in that the Church is precisely a society of men united by mutual love. In some of Ignatius' letters, when he wants to convey to one Church the greeting of another, he uses the expression "the ἀγάπη of the [Syrians, for instance] greets you." In the passage of the letter to the Romans that concerns us, Ignatius is certainly thinking of the preeminence of the Roman Church over the other Churches. This follows, as I have tried to explain, from the verb προκάθηται used a few lines previously to indicate the preeminence of the Church of Rome. Ignatius' expression προκαθημένη τῆς ἀγάπης opens up before our eyes, then, a grandiose vista: the faithful of the universal Church united by the bond of love under the authority of the Church of Rome. And since the verb προκάθησθαι evokes the idea of the banquet and of the one who presides at it, the community of *all* the faithful is transfigured precisely in the image of an ideal eucharistic banquet, in which the Church of Rome occupies the first place.

The superiority of the Church of Rome receives, in the epistle of Ignatius to the Romans, other corroboration. In a subsequent passage he attributes to the Church of Rome the merit of having been a teacher to the others and shows a willingness on his own part to put these teachings into practice ("you have instructed the others, and I do not want that which you prescribe in your teaching to be in vain").[21] And farther on, when he is assailed by the thought of the Syriac Church that he left alone at his departure, he commends her to the prayers of the Romans and declares that from now on the protectors of this diocese, which is now without a pastor, can only be Jesus Christ and, together with him, the Church of Rome animated by charity.[22] Note also here the use, characteristic in Ignatius' writings, of the term ἀγάπη in the sense of Christian community united by the bond of love. But what is especially interesting to us here is the association of the Roman Church with Christ. This suffices to indicate the esteem in which Ignatius held that Church.

But why did Ignatius attribute to her such great dignity? It is likely that the predominant reason was—in Ignatius' mind—the particularly close relation that existed between the Church of Rome and the apostles Peter and Paul. Indeed, Ignatius believed very strongly in the importance of the apostolic tradition. In fact, as it turned out, during the

---

[21] Ignatius, *Letter to the Romans* 3, 1.
[22] Ibid., 9, 1.

stages of his long and wearying voyage from Antioch to Rome, besides writing letters to distant Churches, he preached to the communities with which he came into direct contact; moreover his favorite theme in these discourses was precisely to urge his listeners to remain faithful to the norms established by the apostles, as their only defense in combating the heresies that were starting to spread at that time. In the same letter that he wrote to the Romans he recalls Peter and Paul, declaring that the Roman Church derives her own authority directly from them.[23] This, therefore, is the great privilege upon which, according to Ignatius, the spiritual primacy of Rome is founded.

Speaking of Ignatius, it is also interesting to note that he is the first to apply the title of "Catholic" (καθολική), that is, "universal", to the Church that is made up of all the Churches.[24] And since the Church of Rome had preeminence among all the Christian Churches, it follows, according to Ignatius, and also later on according to Irenaeus, that the concept of "universality" becomes an integral part of the declaration of spiritual primacy.

It is evident, then, that at the beginning of the second century the Church of Rome was—to Ignatius' way of thinking—the first and universal Church and that this opinion (it is easy to argue) must have been shared by all the faithful of the Christian East.

3. The letter of Dionysius, bishop of Corinth, to the Romans

This letter was written to the Christian community at Rome between A.D. 166 and 177, at the time when the chair of

---

[23] Ibid.
[24] Ignatius, *Smyrn.* 8, 2; cf. also *Martyrium Policarpi* 8, 1; 16, 1.

Peter was occupied by Soter. We know of it, as usual, from the invaluable *Ecclesiastical History* of Eusebius, bishop of Caesarea.[25]

Addressing the Church of Rome, Dionysius exalts the charity of that Church, which has a long tradition of coming to the aid of the other Churches in their material and spiritual needs, showing a preference for the most destitute and oppressed, such as those who had been subjected to hard labor in the mines. He assures the Romans, furthermore, that a letter sent from Soter to the Corinthians is being read and reread in that community during the Sunday liturgy. And precisely in this letter of his to the Romans, Dionysius informs us that in addition to the letter of Soter they also read with devotion the much older letter of Clement of which I have already spoken.

At this point we reach the age of Irenaeus. I have already recalled his voyage to Rome to meet with Pope Eleutherius, for the purpose of discussing the thorny question concerning the Montanist heretics, and I have commented upon the famous passage concerning the *potentior principalitas* of the Church of Rome.

4. The Apology of Melito, bishop of Sardis

During the lifetime of Irenaeus, probably in 171 or 172, Melito, bishop of Sardis, sent to the emperor Marcus Aurelius his *Apology*, of which I have already spoken. This is a document in which the ties between the "philosophy" of Melito (that is, Christianity) and the empire are exalted, which

---

[25] Eusebius, *Historia* 4, 23, 9–11.

implies as well the recognition of the spiritual primacy of the Church of Rome.[26]

5. The letter of Polycrates and Irenaeus to Pope Victor

We are now between A.D. 190 and 191. At Rome the chair of Peter is occupied by Pope Victor (189–199), a man of African origin (the first African pope) and of strong character. Shortly after the beginning of his pontificate, certain parties had rekindled the famous controversy that in 151, as I have related, had brought to Rome Polycarp, the venerable bishop of Smyrna: the question concerning the date on which Easter should be celebrated. This time the bishops of Asia, proponents of the Jewish tradition according to which Passover was celebrated on the fourteenth day of the month of Nisan, found an authoritative spokesman in the person of Polycrates, bishop of Ephesus, who in their name had recourse to the pope of Rome. The letter from Polycrates to Victor has been preserved for us in part by the precious *Ecclesiastical History* of Eusebius.[27] In a calm but decisive tone, Polycrates appeals to the uninterrupted tradition and calls as witnesses to it several saintly personages who are laid to rest in the region of Asia, in expectation of the promised resurrection, and, in addition, as many as seven bishops among his own relatives of whom he boasts. On the other hand—he observes—one must hold fast to Sacred Scripture and obey God rather than men. Confronted with such widespread and obstinate dissent, Victor, a strong-willed man who was perhaps influenced also by local demands, decided to hurl an excommunication at the Churches of Asia.[28]

---

[26] See above, p. 22.
[27] Eusebius, *Historia* 4, 24, 1–8.
[28] Ibid., 5, 24, 9.

In this very serious state of affairs, which endangered the unity and harmony of Christians, the wise Irenaeus of Lyons intervened. A decade and a half previously, as you will recall, he had been sent to Rome by his companions in faith for the purpose of obtaining the indulgence of Pope Eleutherius with regard to the Montanist heretics. Now, as a bishop held in great esteem, he did not come to Rome but rather wrote to stern Pope Victor. The letter of Irenaeus, also, has been preserved in large measure by Eusebius.[29] With a view, once more, to maintaining harmony among Christians, Irenaeus affirms that all must accept the Roman usage with regard to the date of Easter, but at the same time he exhorts the pontiff with various arguments to act with moderation, precisely in order to avoid a schism that would do irreparable harm to the Church of Christ.

It is not known precisely what effect the sorrowful and wise words of the bishop of Lyons had on the mind of the pope. Presumably, though, they were helpful in some way. Still, it is true that the same Eusebius, after speaking of the letter of Irenaeus, emphasizes the significance of the latter's name: Εἰρηναῖος, that is, "peaceful".[30] It is certain that there is no further mention of the excommunication of the Eastern Churches or of an eventual schism related to it.

At any rate these events of the last decade of the second century confirm clearly the existence of a spiritual primacy of the Church of Rome in the Christian world. The Churches of Asia, which feel that it is their duty to explain to Pope Victor their perplexity in this matter of worship; the pope, who believes that he has the right to hurl an excommunication against the "dissidents"; the Western bishop, Irenaeus,

---

[29] Ibid., 12–18.
[30] Ibid., 18.

who does not hesitate to call upon the clemency of the Roman pontiff: all this reveals what sort of prestige the Church of Rome had at that time with respect to the other Christian Churches, a prestige that is certainly the equivalent of preeminence.

And now, before moving on to the third century, we find ourselves confronted with an epigraphic document of capital importance.

6. The epigraph of Abercius (figures 1–2)

This inscription is widely known among scholars who study the ancient world. Giovanni Battista De Rossi [1822–1894], the famous Christian archaeologist, described it in this way: "epigramma dignitate et pretio inter christiana facile princeps" [among Christian epigrams easily the most distinguished in dignity and value].[31]

An immense bibliography has accumulated on the subject of this "queen of Christian inscriptions". I myself have contributed to it with two scholarly publications in 1971 and 1973 and with the pages that I dedicated to it in the fourth volume of my *Epigrafia greca*.[32] I do not mind returning today to this theme, with the additional purpose of making more widely known a document that is of the greatest interest for Christian history and spirituality.

Two fragments of the epigraph of Abercius are known, which were discovered in 1883 by the English archaeologist

---

[31] G. B. De Rossi, *Inscriptiones Christianae Urbis Romae*, vol. 2 (Rome, 1888), p. XIII.

[32] M. Guarducci, in *Ancient Society* 2 (1971): 174–203; 4 (1973): 271–79; idem, *Epigrafia greca*, vol. 4 (Rome, 1978), pp. 378–86 (where the most important of the old writings are cited).

William M. Ramsay among the ruins of Hierapolis in Phrygia Salutaris, in Asia Minor. About a decade later, in 1892, when their exceptional importance for the history of Christianity had already been recognized, they were donated by their discoverer to Pope Leo XIII, who in that year was celebrating the fifty-fifth anniversary of his priestly ordination. At first they were displayed in the Museum of Sacred Art at the Lateran; then they went to the Vatican Museum, where they are still found today.

Before examining the epigraph, it is necessary to provide a brief introduction on the circumstances of the famous text.

Long before Ramsay's discovery, we already knew, from a series of manuscripts that can be dated between the tenth and the thirteenth centuries, of a *Vita* [Life] of Abercius, bishop of Hierapolis in Phrygia Salutaris, a *Vita* that was first written down, it seems, as far back as the fourth century. The manuscripts were quite numerous (thirty-seven of them!), an incontestable sign of the importance and the renown of this *Vita*. From it we learn of a singular event. The holy bishop Abercius is said to have been called to Rome to deliver from a demon Lucilla, the daughter of the emperor Marcus Aurelius. After arriving in the city [*urbs*], he expelled the demon that was tormenting the princess, performing the exorcism in the presence of the empress Faustina, while Marcus Aurelius was away from Rome. Then, wishing to mortify even further the evil one whom he had routed, he ordered him to transport to Hierapolis in distant Phrygia a heavy altar made of marble. Upon returning to his homeland, Abercius is said to have used that altar as a stone on which to engrave, before he died, his own epitaph, which he himself dictated.

The fourth-century biographer did not fail to report in the *Vita* the text of this epitaph—twenty-two Greek hexameters—

and added, conscientiously, that in his days some spots on the marble surface were worn smooth, which therefore made it sometimes a bit difficult to read the epigraph.

The story of Lucilla being possessed by the demon and of the emperor who invites to Rome the bishop from the far-off city for the purpose of delivering the princess from the evil one seems, at first glance, like a pious fable. Even less believable, of course, is the bit about the devil being forced by the exorcist to transport the extremely heavy altar from Rome to distant Phrygia. But what are we to think about the trip of Abercius to Rome and about the epitaph that he dictated before he died? Almost all scholars believed that these details, too, were fantastic. I say *almost*, because at least one scholar was an exception. Such was the learned Benedictine monk Giovanni Battista Pitra, who later became a cardinal. In fact, in a study that he wrote in 1855, he emphatically maintained that this mysterious text was genuine.[33] He was entirely correct. About thirty years later, in 1882, the English archaeologist Ramsay, who was excavating in Phrygia Salutaris, discovered the sepulchral inscription of a certain Alexandros, son of Antonios, an epigraph that quoted the first three and last three verses of the much-debated epitaph of Abercius. That epitaph, then, really existed in ancient Hierapolis and must have been well known there some time before several verses from it came to be used in the epitaph of another deceased person. The epigraph of Alexandros, fortunately, could be dated with precision to A.D. 216. In the year following the discovery of Alexandros' epigraph, that is, in 1883, Ramsay then had the good fortune of discovering the two remarkable fragments that, as I said, were then do-

---

[33] J. B. Pitra, *Spicilegium Solesmense*, vol. 2 (Paris, 1855), pp. 332–34, art. 6.

nated by him to Leo XIII and are found now in the Vatican Museum.

Three sides of the ancient altar are preserved in part: the front, the left, and the back. The front side, of which two fragments remain, is taken up by the epigraph (figure 1), the left side presents a crown of that period, carved in relief (figure 2), while the back side is smooth. Of the inscription recorded in the manuscripts, the epigraph that has come down to us contains—in mutilated form—verses 7–15 only. The first verses (1–6)—surely preceded by a heading with the name of the deceased notable—and the last verses (16–22) would have been carved respectively along the top and along the base of the altar, both of them molded. In its entirety, the sepulchral monument of Abercius was very ornate and not unlike others that have come to light in one or another necropolis of Asia Minor. The characters in the inscription suggest a date between A.D. 170 and 200, and this agrees quite well with the information offered in the *Vita* and with the date of the epigraph of Alexandros.

What did Abercius want to write on his tomb?

In the text, to which the *Vita* and the epigraphic discoveries of Ramsay contribute, Abercius speaks in the first person. Essentially, he affirms that he is a disciple of Christ, the chaste pastor with the great eyes that see everything; that he has learned true teachings from him; that he was invited by him to Rome to see "the kingdom and the queen with the golden vesture and the golden shoes"; that he saw there "a people that had a splendid seal"; that he then traveled for a long time in Syria and in Mesopotamia, always accompanied by the spiritual guide of the apostle Paul and surrounded by brothers in the faith; and that he was always nourished with the mystical Fish (Christ), born of God and of the chaste Virgin (Mary), under the form of bread and wine (the Eucharist). At the conclusion, Abercius states that he dictated this, his epitaph, at the age of seventy-two and invited "the one who understands" to pray for him. Then follows the customary threat against those who would violate the tomb: a fine of two thousand gold pieces to be deposited in the treasury of Rome and of one thousand to go to the local government of Hierapolis.

The language, which is deliberately ambiguous, demonstrates that taste for the arcane which was quite widespread then, both among the pagans and also among the Christians. What Abercius said should be understood, as he himself remarks, only by the one who understands, that is, by those who believe in Christ, who are invited to pray for the deceased bishop.

Cloaked in veils of mystery—although they are practically transparent—is also the reference to Rome, which especially interests us here. These are the precise words of Abercius (verses 7–9): "... who [that is, Christ] sent me to Rome to see the kingdom and the queen with the golden vesture and the golden shoes. And I saw there a people that had a splendid seal." [34]

What sort of king is this; who is the queen; and what seal is he talking about?

Abercius is writing between A.D. 170 and 200, evoking the memory of a journey that he made to Rome during the reign of Marcus Aurelius (A.D. 161–180). In those days a great kingdom existed, and Rome was its center. Rome itself was at that time considered a queen and was graced with the title of "golden". As for the people that Abercius had had the

---

[34] Verses 7–9: Εἰς Ῥώμην ὃς ἔπεμψεν ἐμὲν βασιλείαν ἀθρῆσαι / καὶ βασίλισσαν ἰδεῖν χρυσόστολον χρυσοπέδιλον. / λαὸν δ᾽εἶδον ἐκεῖ λαμπρὰν σφραγεῖδαν ἔχοντα.

good fortune of knowing, this was the Roman people, con-
querors of the world, and it is certainly not strange that its
exceptional power was conceived in material terms as a splendid seal imprinted upon it. Yet, if one reflects a little, it is
inconceivable that Christ himself would have sent one of his
bishops to Rome for the specific purpose of becoming acquainted firsthand with the reign of Marcus Aurelius, to con-
template the beauties of the queenly city, and to verify the
power of the Roman people. Beneath the obvious interpretation there must be a deeper meaning that only the ini-
tiate, that is, the Christian, is capable of grasping. The
"kingdom" can be that of Christ on earth, and the "queen
with the golden vesture and the golden shoes" can be understood as the universal Church that has her visible center in
Rome.

It is interesting to note, on this subject, that even before
Abercius the Church is sometimes conceived of as a splendid
queen. Thus, between the end of the first and the beginning
of the second century A.D., a work composed in the envi-
rons of Rome pictures the Church as a royal lady seated on
a throne. I am alluding to the mystical and allegorical "vi-
sions" described in that singular work the *Shepherd of Hermas*.[35] Analogously, a little after the middle of the second
century, at the beginning of the reign of Marcus Aurelius,
Justin (of whom I have already spoken) imagined the Roman Church as a queen upon a throne, wrapped in a gar-
ment of gold.[36] As for the splendid seal that Abercius sees on
the people of Rome, this readily recalls the words of the Letter to the Romans, in which Paul exalts their faith, which is

---

[35] Hermas, *Pastor*, Vis. 1, 2, 2; 2, 5, 1.
[36] Justin, *Dial. Tryph.* 63.

known throughout the world.[37] This exceptional faith can very well be considered as a splendid seal, since "seal", in the language of the ancient Christians, also meant baptism.

By seeking at Rome the "kingdom" and the magnificent "queen" clothed in gold, Abercius shows that he conceives of the Church of Rome as being first among the others and universal and that he aligns himself thereby with the thinking of Ignatius, of Irenaeus, of Melito, and of the other Christian thinkers of the second century. Furthermore, by declaring that Christ himself sent (ἔπεμψεν) him to Rome to see the "kingdom" and the "queen", Abercius shows that he believes that the primacy of the Church of Rome does not depend on the political power of the Romans, but that it is rather a primacy of an exquisitely spiritual character.

7. In the first half of the third century

Crossing the boundaries of the second century and entering upon the third, we encounter the testimony of a great personage: Tertullian.

Born around the middle of the second century in a pagan family, at a certain stage of his life (it is not known exactly when) he converted to Christianity and probably became a priest. Then, feeling that he was inclined toward the heresy of the Montanists, which at that time was spreading through Northern Africa, he ended up becoming one of its followers. This occurred around the year 213. Intelligent, thoroughly versed in Latin and Greek, and with a solid education in the fields of rhetoric, law, and philosophy, he began to write literary works around 197, that is, at a rather late age.

[37] Rom 4:11.

One of the first was in fact a polemical work against the heretics (the treatise *De praescriptione haereticorum*), which was published around the year 200. In this work Tertullian, who was still a Catholic, that is, united with the "universal" Church of Rome, several times has reason to refer to the primacy of the Roman Church. Thus he meditates on the famous passage of the Gospel of Matthew in which Peter is considered the rock upon which Christ will found his Church, the one to whom Christ himself will entrust the keys of the kingdom of heaven;[38] or else he confirms the genuinely apostolic origin of the Church of Rome.[39] In another passage he declares, very significantly, that precisely "from Rome our authority also (that is, that of Christians) is derived" (unde nobis quoque auctoritas praesto est).[40] Later on, after becoming a Montanist, he will not be able to avoid recognizing the primacy of Peter, while still denying this prerogative to the successors of the apostle.

At the beginning of the third century another authoritative voice is raised to affirm the primacy of Peter. It is the voice of Clement of Alexandria.

He was probably born in Athens and then settled in the great cultural center of Alexandria in Egypt, where he studied and also began to teach. Clement left the city at the beginning of the third century, perhaps to avoid the persecution of Septimius Severus, and took refuge in Cappadocia at the home of Alexander, the future bishop of Jerusalem, and died not many years later.

Besides several solid treatises, one of his written works has come down to our time, *Quis dives salvetur?* [What rich man

---

[38] Tertullian, *De praescriptione hereticorum* 22, 4.
[39] Ibid., 32, 2.
[40] Ibid., 36, 2.

will be saved?], which sounds like a sermon intended to demonstrate that, according to Jesus' statement, it is very difficult
for a rich man to obtain eternal salvation. Precisely in this
written work Clement has reason to describe Peter as the
chosen one of Christ, the first of the apostles, and to recall as
a proof of this the episode related in the Gospel of Matthew,
in which Christ ordered Peter to pay the tribute for himself
and for the Master with the stater [Greek coin] that was found
in the mouth of the first fish that had taken the bait, a sign of
the extremely close bond that would exist, by the will of
Christ, between him and his chief disciple.[41]

Between the end of the second and the middle of the third
century the figure of Origen of Alexandria loomed large
over Christian literature. I have already recalled that, around
the year 215, he too made the ritual voyage to Rome so as to
become acquainted firsthand with that famous Church.[42] No
wonder, then, that some thoughts of his concerning the spiritual primacy of the Roman Church have come down to us
as well.

Born a Christian at Alexandria in Egypt, and endowed
with intellectual intensity and eloquence, he was a famous
Christian scholar and in particular a teacher whose instruction was much sought-after. Even personages of the most
distinguished lineage wanted to learn from him. Suffice it to
mention Julia Mamaea—the well-educated mother of the
emperor Alexander Severus, who called him to Antioch, the
city to which she had followed her son during the war against
the Persians[43]—and, later on, the emperor Philip "the Arab"

[41] Clement of Alexandria, *Quis dives salvetur?* 21. The Gospel passage is
Matthew 17:27.
[42] See above, p. 14.
[43] Eusebius, *Historia* 5, 12, 3.

and his wife, the empress Severa, to whom Origen wrote letters.[44] Origen's life, which was troubled and embittered by disagreements with the episcopate of Alexandria, with which he was finally reconciled, unfolded between Egypt and the Syro-Palestinian region. In his old age he was not spared the terrible trial of the persecution of Decius (250), during which he was imprisoned and tortured and which he survived by three years, concluding his days then at Tyre (253).

For Origen, too, Peter is the "great foundation", the "most firm rock" upon which Christ founded his Church. This can be read in the homily on the book of Exodus, one of the homilies that he composed after the year A.D. 230 in Palestine.[45] He develops the argument, as is only logical, with reference to the famous passage found in the Gospel of Matthew.[46] But of particular significance for Origen's thought concerning the spiritual primacy of the Church of Rome are the words written by him around the year 246, in his refutation of the Neoplatonic philosopher Celsus.[47] Here Origen develops the thesis—already maintained, as we have seen, by Melito, the bishop of Sardis—that there is a providential relationship between the empire and the Church. The unity of the empire and the universal peace brought about by Augustus [Caesar] have favored the spread of Christ's Church; and since Rome is the center of the empire, Origen, too, comes to admit that Rome is, furthermore, the center of the universal Church and holds the primacy among all the other Christian Churches.

---

[44] Ibid., 36, 3.

[45] Origen, *In Exodum* 5, 4 (in *Patrologia Latina* 12, 329). See also Eusebius, *Historia* 5, 25, 8.

[46] Mt 12:10–14, 31.

[47] Origen, *Contra Celsum* 2, 30.

An indirect proof of the spiritual primacy that at Origen's time was attributed to the Church of Rome emerges then from an episode involving Origen himself. Shortly after 230, during a journey through Palestine, Origen had been ordained a priest by local bishops without his knowing it. This ordination did not please the Church of Alexandria, headed then by Bishop Demetrius, who was not kindly disposed toward Origen, so that the latter was condemned by a synod of bishops that was convened on that occasion. The bishops of Asia Minor, who knew and appreciated Origen, took no notice of the condemnation. On the other hand, the Church of Rome did take note of it and ratified it through the mouth of Pontian, who was pope then (230–235).[48]

The Church of Alexandria, therefore, had sensed the obligation, in a question concerning Christianity in the Eastern world, to have recourse as well and above all to the great Church of the West, whose authority she recognized, and it is certain that Rome's assent to her condemnation of Origen must have been pleasing to her.

8. Conclusion

Summing up, we must declare that between the end of the first and the middle of the third century, that is, in the times closest to the appearance of Christianity, the spiritual primacy of the Church of Rome was generally recognized throughout the Christian world. The recognition of the primacy was then accompanied by the acknowledgment of her universality. The Church of Rome, and she alone, was the universal Church, the Church of Christ.

---

[48] This is attested by a passage from Saint Jerome (*Epist.* 33, 4).

Among the other voices that are raised to declare this, those from the Christian world of the East are impressive. These are joined then by the very significant voice of Irenaeus, a figure of great authority who belongs both to the East, where his formation took place, and also to the West, where he later did his pastoral work. The explicit declarations of these exponents of Christianity are then confirmed implicitly, in the year 155, by the initiative of Polycarp, bishop of Smyrna, who in order to resolve the difficult question of the date of the Paschal celebration felt it was his duty to travel—despite considerable difficulties—to Rome, for the purpose of conferring with Pope Anicetus.

We have seen, furthermore, that Irenaeus recognized the *potentio principalitas* of the Church of Rome and sought to explain it, finding the reasons for it in her greatness, her importance, her renown, her foundation through the work of Peter and Paul, and her universality based upon the providential universality of the empire. Outstanding among these reasons, because of its concreteness, is the foundation of this Church by the work of the two apostles.

In reality, to be more precise, the great reason seems to be, in the final analysis, the real presence at Rome of the tombs of the two apostles and especially that of Peter, the apostle chosen by Christ to be the foundation of his Church.

2

AN INTERVAL OF CENTURIES

With Origen we have arrived at about the middle of the
third century. Now I propose to illustrate the "primacies" of
the Church of Rome, "primacies" that continue to this day
and that are the consequence, confirmation, and proof of
that ancient primacy.

But between the middle of the third century and our era
there is an interval of many centuries. We cannot proceed
without taking this interval into consideration as well, with
respect (of course) to the problem that is of interest here: the
problem, I mean to say, of the spiritual primacy of the Roman Church. During those centuries, indeed, the Church
experienced memorable events, some of which were related,
directly or indirectly, to the primacy.

At the middle of the third century the persecutions that
had afflicted the Christian communities at intervals, starting
from the first century, had not yet come to an end; the final
and—comparatively speaking—most severe persecution, that
of Diocletian, had not yet begun. Furthermore, the Church
had not yet vanquished all of the heresies that had arisen in
her own bosom until the end of the first century, and these
heresies had been and were a danger to the unity and also,
implicitly, to the primacy of the Church of Rome, the faithful custodian of the true doctrine. The danger was noticed
quite promptly, and it was in reality very serious, so much so
that in the second century Irenaeus, the bishop of Lyons, felt

obliged, as we have seen, to write one of his voluminous works about it.[1]

On the subject of the heresies, it will not be inappropriate to recall that the oldest and most important among them were derived above all from Gnosis, a doctrine that sought salvation in the knowledge of God, γνῶσις and fed on various elements drawn from classical mythology, from the mystery religions, or even from the Bible. Later, on the other hand, heretical speculations would move about in purely theological areas, concerning the essence of the Trinity and the Person of Christ.

In the course of the second century, as I have already mentioned, exponents of various heretical sects had made their way to Rome, drawn not only by the fascination of the capital city that ruled the world, but also (as we might well believe) by the fascination of the universal Church that had her seat precisely in Rome.[2]

In the first half of the third century (ca. 200–238, from the pontificate of Zephyrinus to that of Fabian), trinitarian and christological heresies, also, were coming into the limelight at Rome that then, between the fourth and the fifth centuries, would manifest themselves more clearly elsewhere. In the middle of the third century, however, Christians at Rome still remembered those previous heretical developments that not so long before had stirred up dissension and provoked condemnations.

The heresies were, without a doubt, harmful to the spiritual primacy of the Roman Church, but what proved to be even more harmful was a phenomenon that began to be observed precisely in Rome around the middle of the third

[1] See above, pp. 17–19.
[2] See above, pp. 15–16, 33–34.

century, during the pontificate of Stephen I. I mean the
gradual passage of the primacy from the Church of Rome
(understood as an entity governed by the bishop and by the
priests) to the person of the bishop alone. We can infer this
new situation from a phrase that later on, in the first half of
the fourth century, was penned by a pagan historian, Ammianus Marcellinus. At a certain point in his *History* he
states, indeed, as something known to all, that "the bishops
of the Eternal City enjoy a much greater authority."[3] It is
not difficult to note here an echo of the *potentior principalitas* of which Irenaeus had spoken,[4] with this difference: the
text of Irenaeus speaks about the Church of Rome, not
about the bishop.

The transfer of authority from the Church to the bishop
was accompanied by the gradual change of the official language from Greek to Latin, a change that no doubt played
its part in the future separation of Constantinople from
Rome.[5]

With the advent of the seventh century, a danger from the
East confronted the Roman Church and all of Christianity:
the expansion of the Islamic religion. Founded by Muhammad, who was believed to be the last prophet, it spread
rapidly in the Arab world and beyond the boundaries thereof.
After the death of the prophet (632), the Arabs, bringing
with them the new faith, together with a new language
and a new, unique culture, invaded Northern Africa; then,
after crossing the Strait of Gibraltar, they reached the Iberian Peninsula. Here their first headquarters was Granada.

---

[3] Ammianus Marcellinus, *Rerum gestarum libri* 15, 10.
[4] See above, pp. 18–19.
[5] See below, p. 53.

Later on they sought to establish a footing in other localities in Europe, in France, and in Italy. Halted in France at Poitiers in 733 by Charles Martel and then elsewhere by other Christian armies, the Arabs left more lasting traces of their presence in Sicily, where they then applied themselves to the business of piracy. The final act of the centuries-long Arab adventure in Europe would be the capitulation of the Arab emirate of Granada to the army of Isabella of Castile and Ferdinand the Catholic. The besieged city surrendered on January 2 in the year 1492. A few months later (it is interesting to note), Christopher Columbus would set sail, precisely from the Iberian Peninsula, to discover that new world which would open new paths for the Christian apostolate.

If the seventh century started to pit the Church against the Arabs and the religion of which they were the bearers, in the following century began a phenomenon that proved to be detrimental to the spiritual primacy of the Roman Church. I am referring to the institution of the temporal power of the popes, a power that necessarily affected their freedom of judgment and of action and consequently diminished the prestige their words enjoyed among the faithful.

According to a widely known tradition, the first property was transferred to the Church by Constantine. The document on which the tradition is based is a letter from the emperor to Pope Sylvester. We learn from it that Constantine, afflicted with leprosy, had been cured and baptized by the pontiff and that out of gratitude Constantine had presented to him the famous donation. This is said to have consisted of a palace in the city of Rome and one in every single province of Italy. This is the famous donation to which Dante alludes, deploring the fact, in the well-known verses from the *Inferno*:[6]

> *Ahi, Costantin, di quanto mal fu matre*
> *Non la tua conversion ma quella dote*
> *Che da te prese il primo ricco patre.*

But the suggestive letter from Constantine to the first "Wealthy Father" [as opposed to "Holy Father"], that is, to Pope Sylvester I, does not pass through the sieve of historical investigation.[7] It was forged in the times when the popes in fact lived in a grand palace (the Lateran) and when Rome and a part of Italy were in fact in their possession; and it probably was meant to justify the power that the Church had acquired. As for Constantine, though, and his relation with the Church herself, we can only say that the Church received from him great benefices and that after peace was made with the empire, she came to know for the first time, as we will see, imperial pomp and even adopted several characteristic aspects of it.[8]

In order to find the Church in possession of a temporal power, that is, of a territory that is geographically and politically well defined, we must proceed to 756. In that year, indeed, Pepin, king of the Franks, having made himself the protector of the Church against the threat of the Lombards headed by Aistulf, finally defeated the barbarian invaders and then ceded to the Church, as her permanent possession, the

---

[6] Dante, *Inferno*, 19, 115–17: "Alas, Constantin, it was the mother of so much evil! Not your conversion, but that gift Which was taken from you by the first 'Wealthy Father'."

[7] Cf. A. Hamman, in *Dizionario Patristico*, vol. 1 (Casale Monferrato, 1983), col. 1031 (article "Donazione di Costantino" [Donation of Constantine]).

[8] See below, pp. 74–75.

exarchate of Ravenna, which in 751 the Lombards had taken from the Byzantines.

It is interesting to recall, in this connection, that in 756, while the Lombards still had Rome under siege, Pope Stephen II sent from the besieged city anguished calls for help to his friend, King Pepin. One of these letters—the third—is effectively contrived to read as though it had been written by Peter himself: "I, Peter, God's Apostle, who have you as my adopted sons [the Franks were considered by the pope as adopted sons of the Church], exhort you to defend from the hands of our adversaries this city of Rome and the people committed by God to me and to snatch the house in which I rest, according to the flesh, away from the contamination of the barbarians." In his commentary upon this epistle, Ferdinand Gregorovius, the famous historian of medieval Rome, believed that he had discovered here a literary fiction of the pope who was writing. On the contrary, the text contains a sincere and dramatic appeal to the apostle, whose tomb was located in the caves beneath the Vatican basilica, the pride of the city and the guarantee of safety for the Church.[9]

Peter, thus providentially invoked, then urged Pepin to liberate the city, and to it the victorious king granted, in addition, the foremost temporal authority. Such a concession, on the other hand, did not fail to stir up conflicts between Rome and Constantinople over the ownership of the exarchate of Ravenna, disputes that were embittered by the struggle against the veneration of images (iconoclasm), which raged in the East and to which Rome, on the other hand, was opposed. But that first temporal power ended up being kept by Rome and was maintained, with additions and modifications, through long

---

[9] Cf. O Bertolini, *Roma di fronte a Bisanzio e ai Longobardi* (Bologna, 1941), p. 567.

centuries. Its disappearance or, I should say, its drastic and definitive limitation did not take place until 1929. But I will speak of this historic event later on.[10]

After the eighth century the spiritual primacy of the Church of Rome, gradually weakened by the negative factors that I have mentioned, was put to a difficult test by an event that was quite serious, both in itself and also because of the consequences that followed from it: the separation of the Church of Constantinople from the Church of Rome.

If heresies had produced more or less deep scratches in the unity of the Church, this separation was the first real cut, strictly speaking, the first great blow struck both against the unity of the Church and, consequently, against the spiritual primacy of Rome.

This result came about between the ninth and the eleventh century.

The first conflicts between Rome and Constantinople arose in the ninth century and had as their protagonists the pope of Rome, Nicholas I, and the patriarch of Constantinople, Photius. There were various reasons for the disputes. There was, first of all, Rome's protest concerning the illegitimate manner in which Photius succeeded Ignatius as patriarch (the latter had been forced to resign). Photius, in turn, expressed reservations concerning the authority of the pontiff. The dispute then extended to the famous formula of the Creed concerning the Holy Spirit: *qui ex Patre Filioque procedit* [who proceeds from the Father and the Son]. Photius, indeed, and his followers maintained that the Spirit proceeded from the Father only and claimed that the *Filioque* was a heretical

[10] See below, p. 67.

addition. These differences, however, did not prevent Photius from being reconciled with the Church of Rome in the council held at Constantinople in the Basilica of Santa Sophia (November 17, 879–March 13, 880).

But the fire was smoldering beneath the ashes. The disagreements were rekindled in the eleventh century. This time the protagonists were Pope Leo IX, and Patriarch Michael Cerularius. The Church of Constantinople had seen fit to criticize certain customs of the Church of Rome, such as the fast on the sabbath day [Saturday] and the use of azymous, that is, unleavened bread in the eucharistic celebration. At Constantinople, in contrast, it was the custom (and it still is in the Orthodox Church) to distribute leavened bread to the faithful who are gathered around the sacred banquet table. Although we must admit that such reasons had in those days a certain importance, it is clear that behind them there continued to be, as at the time of Photius, a general aversion to the authority of the Church of Rome. In order to allay the disagreements, the pope sent a suitable legation to Constantinople in 1054, but in vain. Nothing at all was accomplished by the meeting, which ended in mutual excommunications!

To exhaust the subject of the unfortunate rupture between Rome and Constantinople, we might add that the relations between the two Churches became still worse, if that is possible, during the thirteenth century, when—following the Fourth Crusade—the Latin empire of the East was established (1204–1261).[11] The rift became even deeper, al-

---

[11] I will speak later on about the dramatic flight from Constantinople of the last Latin emperor of the West, Baldwin II, who reputedly salvaged, as he fled, the precious head of the Virgin, *Hodigitria*, which today is incorporated, after rather romantic adventures, into the great Marian icon of Montevergine near Avellino (see below, pp. 99–100).

though the Byzantine emperors, frightened by the growing threat of a Turkish invasion, tried to encourage a reconciliation that (they hoped, at least) would obtain a guarantee of military assistance from the West. Let it be noted that the council that took place in Ferrara and in Florence between 1438 and 1439 was of little use in reestablishing peace between the two Churches; it was followed about fifteen years later (1453) by the historic conquest of Constantinople by the Turks. It was not until 1965 that the anachronistic excommunications of 1054 were repealed!

Shortly after this excommunication, in the second half of the eleventh century, the Church of Rome found herself in the midst of a conflict that seriously endangered her spiritual authority: the so-called battle of investitures.

The German emperors had arrogated to themselves the right of intervening in the investiture of high ecclesiastical offices, which led more than once to scandalous acts of simony. Such a state of affairs was opposed with unbending determination by the virtuous monk Hildebrand, who was born not far from Siena, was educated in the famous French monastery of Cluny, and in 1073 became Pope Gregory VII. His battle for the *libertas ecclesiae* [freedom of the Church] culminated in the period between 1070 and 1080, a decade filled with memorable events, among which stands out the incident in which the emperor Heinrich IV, who had been excommunicated by the pontiff, came repentant to implore his forgiveness, in mid-winter 1077, while Gregory was staying at Canossa as the guest of the Countess Mathilda of Tuscany.

The battle over investitures continued throughout the eleventh century and into the beginning of the twelfth, until—in the year 1122—a concordat signed at Worms during the pontificate of Callistus II began to regulate the painful situation: to the emperor belonged the right of feudal investiture, whereas spiritual investiture, expressed in the conferral of the ring and the crozier, was reserved to the Church and to her alone. The Church of Rome, then, in essence, had won the battle.

Even before the battle of investitures was over, the period of the Crusades began (1095–1229): the five famous expeditions promoted by the Christians of the West in order to liberate the holy places of Palestine from the impious occupation of the infidels. These were the Seljuk Turks [in Asia Minor], a people of the Islamic religion who, having taken possession of the land of Jesus, were tormenting the Christian pilgrims who devotedly set out to visit it, and in particular to venerate the Holy Sepulcher. The first invitation to take part in this pious enterprise was issued by Pope Urban II in 1095; and four years later, in 1099, the army of Godfrey of Bouillon, the "captain" of whom Torquato Tasso sings in the poem *Gerusalemme liberata*, actually liberated the holy city from the infidels—not without great sacrifices. The goal had finally been attained, but the conquest was not lasting.

All in all, the undertaking of the Crusades—in which the pious intention that had originally promoted them gradually became entangled with other motives of another sort—can be considered as a European reaction to the wave of Muslims that had mobilized against Europe. Although they did not reach their intended goal, the definitive liberation of the Holy Land, the Crusades had a remarkable political and economic importance in the history of the peoples who came in contact with one another during them.

The Church of Rome, to be sure, derived from them a certain advantage as to her prestige. The invitation issued by Urban II and confirmed (it is obvious) more or less decisively by his successors increased, in fact—in a common religious ideal—the cohesiveness of the faithful who deferred to the Roman Church.

Following the course of the thirteenth century, after the period of the Crusades, and crossing the threshold of the fourteenth, we must acknowledge that the so-called exile in Avignon, that is, the transfer of the papal see from Rome to France, did not really help the cause of the primacy of Rome. This painful exile lasted, practically speaking, from 1305 to 1377. In favor of it was, above all, the king of France, Philip the Fair, who wanted to have close at hand a force as mighty as the papacy, and his will naturally gained the support of the French prelates. The fact is that in 1305 the bishop of Bordeaux was elected pope with the name of Clement V and remained in France, where he had been elected; four years later, in 1309, he established his residence in Avignon. The choice of this noble city as a papal residence was determined especially by the fact that Avignon had been under the rule of the Holy See since 1229.

In the sumptuous palace in Avignon other popes succeeded one another. Some of them perceived the call of Rome and the duty to return to the see of Peter, while from Italy arose anguished appeals to come back. But only in 1377 did Pope Gregory XI decide to leave Avignon to return permanently to the Eternal City. An important role in this decision, as is well known, was played by the supplications of an elect lady, Saint Catherine of Siena.

Gregory died shortly after his return, in 1378, and his death signaled the beginning of a period of enormous confusion for the Church of Rome, during which popes and antipopes vied with one another. This was the Great Schism.

The Great Schism, too, kept the successors of Peter far from Rome almost constantly and was, like the exile in

Avignon, harmful to the cause of the primacy. Only after the Council of Constance (1415–1417) did the permanent installation of Martin I in Rome procure for the Church a period of relative tranquility.

Notwithstanding the exile in Avignon and the Great Schism, and other incidents that were not at all favorable, the spiritual primacy of the Church of Rome remained very strong in the West until the end of the Middle Ages.[12] It was, after all, a church that, anchored to faith in Christ and to the chair of Peter, had resisted in her day, together with the empire, the invasions of the barbarian; that, when the empire fell in 476, survived it, inheriting from it the essential elements of civilization; and that for centuries was, despite the errors attributable to the fragility of human nature, a beacon of wisdom, of culture, and of sanctity. Her word, therefore, had to be listened to and followed.

But with the advent of the sixteenth century new clouds threatened to darken—in the West—the heavens over the Church.

The clouds bore the name of "Reformation".

The first figure who opposed the Church of Rome under this name was Martin Luther. Born in Germany, at Eisleben, in 1483, Luther was an intelligent man but prone to emotional outbursts and arrogance. He entered the Augustinian Order, pronounced his solemn vows in 1506, and in the following year became a priest. As such he stayed in Rome between 1510 and 1511, charged by his monastery

---

[12] When speaking of the West, we must naturally exclude Carthage, which however had played such a great role in the history of early Christianity. Indeed, Carthage and all of northern Africa had been in the power of the Arabs for centuries.

to register a protest with the Holy See. At that time Julius II was pope. At the sight of the Renaissance splendor of the papal court Luther was disgusted. To this reason for his aversion others were added after his return to Germany; prominent among these reasons was the traffic in indulgences for the benefit of the deceased. So it came about that the rebel monk very soon reached the point where he considered the papacy an institution of the devil and saw in the Roman pontiff the Antichrist in person. Such sentiments dictated the famous manifesto of ninety-five theses that, in 1517, Luther posted on the door of the Wittenberg cathedral (according to the custom of the times), a manifesto in which, besides deploring certain obvious abuses, he also attacked vehemently certain fundamental principles of Christian doctrine. Excommunicated in 1520, he gained the support of powerful German personages who were hostile toward the Church of Rome and continued fearlessly for the rest of his life, in his preaching and in his writings, to fight against Rome and to declare heresy everything that did not square with his own opinions, which he held as dogmas of faith.

All told, the work of Luther separated from the Church of Rome a large part of Germany and of the Scandinavian countries. Luther died in 1545; but even before his death the winds of the Reformation had overrun other European countries as well.

The first to enter into the whirlwind was England. There, in 1533, King Henry VIII made, as everyone knows, memorable decisions. The husband of Catherine of Aragon, he wanted to break off that marriage so as to wed a new wife, Anne Boleyn, whom he then—please note—had killed (and she was not the only one!) ... Because the Holy See, naturally, refused to give its consent to the divorce from

Catherine, Henry VIII had the subservient Parliament approve a series of measures on the basis of which a new Church was established, having as its visible head the king (or the queen) of England.

This "act of supremacy" meant a break with the Church of Rome. The schism had grave consequences: the suppression of thriving monasteries, whose lands obviously went to enrich the crown and the nobility, and above all the persecution of the Catholics who remained faithful to the Church of Rome. Even the great cathedrals erected in England by the Catholics during the Middle Ages suffered damage to their precious marble furnishings.

After Henry VIII the persecution of Catholics abated during the reign of Mary Tudor, who was a Catholic, but in 1559 it was reaffirmed with utter ruthlessness by the new queen, Elizabeth I. At that time the conflicts between Protestants and Catholics were renewed, accompanied by severe persecutions.

After England, it was Switzerland. There, following in the footsteps of Luther, the theologian John Calvin (1509–1564) took sides against the Catholic Church. Of French origin (he had been born at Noyon, in France), Calvin spent a large part of his career at Geneva, in Switzerland. His doctrine was, essentially, that of Luther. However he propounded certain details of it with greater precision, for instance, their pet theory of predestination. The Calvinist movement became widespread, not only in Switzerland, but also in France, in Holland, and in England. In this last-mentioned country the Puritans (so the Calvinists came to be called) had influence especially upon the common people and the bourgeois, and not so much upon the upper class, although Queen Elizabeth personally showed sympathy toward the Calvinist movement.

How did the Church of Rome react—we might now ask—when faced with the Reformation and with the painful schisms that the latter had provoked?

Church officials began, as we have seen, with the excommunication of Luther in 1520. Scarcely seven years had elapsed from this date when Rome was struck—in 1527—by an enormous calamity: the sack of the city at the hands of the *Landsknechte*, [German mercenaries] maneuvered by the emperor Charles V. Once this scourge had passed, the Catholic Church, preoccupied with the increasingly serious damage being done by the Reformation, devoted herself energetically to organizing her own Counter-Reformation. And it was indeed a grandiose movement, a leaven in the mass of dough, in which the active participants were not only the hierarchy of the Church but also the entire faithful people. All of the nobler elements in the Church made their particular intellectual or practical contributions in every field: religion, culture, law, and art.

This ardent reaction culminated in the Council of Trent, which opened in 1545, the very year in which Luther died. It was convened by Pope Paul III with the inaugural bull *Laetare Hierusalem*, was concluded in 1563, and continued with its additional sessions up till the beginning of the seventeenth century.

The Counter-Reformation naturally increased the prestige of the Church of Rome. An even greater increase was brought about in 1571 by the splendid victory that the Catholics carried off at Lepanto (in ancient times known as Naupaktos, in the gulf of Corinth) against the Turkish fleet. Descendants of tribes from the heart of Asia, they were, like the Arabs, followers of the Muslim religion. Already in the eleventh century they were to be found in Asia Minor, and they gradually grew in strength and daring to the point where in 1453 they succeeded in conquering no less than the great city of Constantinople. After establishing themselves permanently in the capital of the empire, they aimed (obviously) to extend their own dominion far and wide. Their strength was in their fleet, and they began to sail along all the shipping routes of the Mediterranean as plunderers, under the aegis of Muhammad, so as to constitute a new and extremely grave danger for the Church of Rome and for the entire Catholic West. But they were stopped at Lepanto by that famous victory of October 7, 1571, which Pope Pius V, who initiated the undertaking, attributed to the intercession of the Blessed Virgin.

The Church of Rome entered the eighteenth century reinvigorated. During that period she had to witness the so-called "wars of religion", the sad consequences of the Reformation, wars in which Protestants and Catholics, led by various political interests, fought against each other, especially in France and in Germany. On the other hand, thanks to the vast colonial undertakings of Spain and France, the Catholic Church greatly expanded her own work of evangelization in America and in Asia. Furthermore, it was granted to her to win another decisive victory over the Turks in the battle of Vienna, which was fought on September 12, 1683, under the auspices of Pope Innocent XI. The victory, which was also attributed to the intercession of Mary, rescued the Catholic Church from another very serious danger. Just as the victory at Lepanto had stopped the Turks by sea, so too the victory at Vienna stopped them on land. The Turks were forced to renounce their yearned-for expansion in Europe, which implied giving up the goal that was at the pinnacle of their hopes: that of conquering Rome.

Difficult trials awaited the Roman Church in the eighteenth century. They can be summed up in the word "Enlightenment". As you know, this refers to a movement that pervaded all of Europe, on account of which the eighteenth century has been called precisely "the century of lights" (*le siècle des lumières*). The movement hinged upon an absolute respect for reason, which, at a certain point, became thoroughly transfigured into a divine being: the goddess Reason. Based upon this principle, it ended up taking into consideration only those things that did not transcend the limits of the human intellect, therefore refuting all revelation. This meant, in practice, atheism. In this way a widespread laicization came about, which involved many states in Europe. The movement also provided an impulse toward that memorable and enormously important event, the French Revolution, which erupted in 1789.

Resolutely opposed to the basic principles of Catholicism, and of Christianity in general, the Enlightenment (obviously) diminished the power and prestige of the Church of Rome.

The French Revolution was succeeded—between the end of the eighteenth and the second decade of the nineteenth century—by the period dominated by the grand figure of Napoleon Bonaparte.

This, too, was a very trying time for the Church of Rome. Passing over numerous events that were also of great importance, I will limit myself to mentioning only those that pertain more or less directly to the Church of Rome.

We should observe, first of all, that the relations between Napoleon and the Roman Church were certainly not the best. Aware that he was an exceptional man, destined for great enterprises, Napoleon nevertheless perceived in the Church a superhuman power, which sometimes induced him to show, if not respect, then at least tolerance. But, in effect, his hostility prevailed almost always over his benevolence.

In 1797, after the tumultuous victories that he won in northern Italy, Napoleon, still General Bonaparte, humiliated Pope Pius VI with the Treaty of Tolentino (February 19). The following year, when the Roman Republic had been established, the pope himself was taken prisoner by the French and deported to France, where he died one year later, "a prisoner of the state", as a result of the enormous hardships of the journey. And it took some doing to have his remains transported in 1800 from Valenza (the place of his death) to Rome: an act of "generosity" carried out by order of Napoleon himself.

Another reason that probably induced him to carry out this act was the election of the successor to Pius VI. Indeed, the new pope, Pius VII, was not at all a pliable man, and furthermore he had at his side an intelligent and energetic secretary, Cardinal Ercole Consalvi. In 1801, when Napoleon was already first consul, a concordat was reached between the Holy See and France. This allowed the pope to travel to Paris in 1804 to confer upon Napoleon the imperial crown. Except that, at the very moment of the ceremony, which took place with great solemnity on December 2 of that year in the church of Notre Dame, Napoleon took the crown from him and put it on his head by himself. After which he crowned by his own hand his wife, Josephine Beauharnais. Nor was this the only humiliation that the Roman pontiff had to suffer during his stay in Paris. But the worst was yet to come.

In 1809, having created the Italian Republic, Napoleon excluded Rome from it, incorporating it instead into the French empire, and he declared that the temporal power had become thoroughly obsolete. Pius VII was arrested in his palace, the Quirinal, and deported to France. Here Napoleon, wishing to dissolve his own marriage with Josephine, obliged the pope to grant his wish in the humiliating Concordat of Fontainebleau (January 25, 1813), which was retracted immediately after by the pope. Debased by the will of Napoleon practically to the level of an imperial chaplain, Pius VII was finally liberated and, after so many misfortunes, reentered Rome triumphantly on May 24, 1814.

In 1815, after the defeat of Napoleon at Waterloo and his exile to the little island of Saint Helena, the Restoration procured for the Roman Church a period of relative peace.

But now the repercussions of the liberal revolt pervaded Europe and spread even to Italy and to Rome. The ephemeral Roman Republic (February 9–July 3, 1849) was founded in the city. Pius IX, who at that time sat upon the chair of Peter, could not tolerate the situation that had been created in Rome, and by the end of 1848 he had abandoned the city to take refuge in Gaeta under the protection of the king of Naples. He returned to Rome only in 1850, escorted by the French, who had set up a regime in the city (the Roman Republic had meanwhile been abolished). They then maintained a garrison for twenty years, until 1870, except for a brief interval between 1866 and 1867, the latter being the year in which they conquered Garibaldi in the battle of Mentana.

After returning to Rome in 1850, Pius IX showed an increasing willingness to fight for the defense of the Roman Church, in the exalted awareness of her universality and her spiritual primacy. He gave evidence of these sentiments in 1867, when, taking advantage also of the opportune absence of the French, he ordered grandiose celebrations for what was believed to be the eighteenth centenary of the martyrdom of the apostles (in reality the year of martyrdom was, at least for Peter, A.D. 64). On that same occasion, Pius IX commanded a solemn opening of the bronze case that—inside the Vatican basilica—encloses the precious *wooden chair of Saint Peter*, a symbol of the teaching authority of the Church and, what is very important, announced the First Vatican Council for the year 1869.[13]

After two years had passed, it actually opened and was distinguished for its proclamation of the dogma of the primacy and infallibility of the pope. The Roman Church had reached an apogee of her prestige. Except that, while the Council was still carrying on its work, on September 20, 1870, the troops of General Raffaele Cadorna entered Rome through the breach at Porta Pia, suddenly joining those of General Nino Bixio, which descended from the heights of the Gianicolo. Rome had become the capital of the new Kingdom of Italy. After the occupation of Rome, the Council continued its work for another month; it was suspended (not closed) on October 20. Meanwhile Pius IX had retired with his court into the Vatican, within the circle of the Leonine Walls, abandoning to the Italians his other two official residences: the Patriarchio beside the Lateran basilica and the palace of the Quirinal.

A voluntary "prisoner" in the Vatican, Pius IX died there in 1878, and four of his successors continued in the same "seclusion": Leo XIII, Pius X, Benedict XV, and Pius XI. In these long years of "imprisonment", the Holy See still main-

---

[13] On this subject of the grandiose ceremonies of 1867, which attracted to Rome, as it seems, an enormous number of the faithful, and among them distinguished high-ranking prelates—not only from Italy, France, and Spain, but also from the Far East and Africa—I wish to mention the vivid description of the German historian Ferdinand Gregorovius, who at that very time happened to be in Rome. F. Gregorovius, *Wanderjahre in Italien*, vol. 4, 3d ed. (Leipzig, 1876), pp. 325–27; idem, *Römische Tagebücher* (Stuttgart, 1892), pp. 360ff.

tained contacts with the faithful in Italy and abroad, with the world of culture, and with some foreign states. We cannot overlook, moreover, with respect to that period, the great figure of Leo XIII (1878–1903), the immediate successor of Pius IX. With his two encyclicals, *Libertas* and *Rerum novarum*, Leo XIII, demonstrating keen intelligence and almost prophetic foresight, applied to the modern world the social doctrine of the Church.

Finally, in 1929, during the pontificate of Pius XI, came the Lateran Treaty, reconciling the papacy with Italy. On the basis of this treaty, the Church lost the greater part of her territories, but what she retained—the Vatican and the adjacent lands—was enough to make her an independent and sovereign entity that was well defined geographically and politically. In short, the city-state of the Vatican was established. With that a unique situation was created: not so much that of a little state inserted into a larger state (there have been other examples of that) as that of a sovereign city encompassed within another city.

The almost total loss of her temporal power (we must acknowledge) was to the Church's advantage. That loss meant the removal of an impediment that, as I have already said, had from 756 on affected the free expansion of the Church herself as a universal, that is, "catholic" power in the true sense of the word.

Following the course of the years since the Lateran Treaty, we can fix our sights upon the renowned personage of Pius XII, who led the Church through the difficulties of the Second World War; who, with his prestige and with his tireless work, won for the Church herself the respect of the entire world; who, among other things, made the heroic decision to open to scientific investigation the subterranean passages of the Vatican basilica—which until then had been a mystery—in which (I repeat his own words) the foundations of the Christian faith are found.

Finally we should recall the Second Vatican Council, opened by John XXIII in 1962 and concluded by Paul VI in 1965. In this council they did not speak of dogmas, as in Vatican I, but rather confronted and set out to solve problems regarding the pastoral work of the Church in the modern world.

We have thus arrived at our era. The universal Church of Rome has remained, through the centuries and the vicissitudes of history, alive and still vital. She numbers millions and millions of faithful throughout the world, many of whom the Roman pontiff often travels to visit in far-off lands and even more often receives and blesses in the Vatican.

Figure 1. The epigraph of Abercius (Vatican Museum).

Figure 2. The altar of Abercius, left side (Vatican Museum).

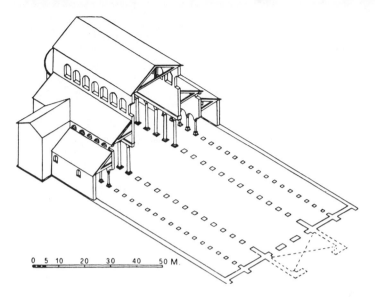

Figure 3. Rome, Saint John Lateran, the Constantine Basilica, reconstruction (Krautheimer-Corbett; architectural drawing by J. B. Lloyd).

Figure 4. Lateran Baptistery, two-pillared atrium [*atrio a forcipe*] from the time of Sixtus III (fifth century; from *San Giovanni in Laterano*, edited by Carlo Pietrangeli).

Figure 5. Lateran Baptistery, decoration in *opus sectile* of the atrium from the time of Sixtus III (fifth century; from *San Giovanni in Laterano*, edited by Carlo Pietrangeli).

Figure 6. Portrait of Christ in the catacomb of Commodilla.

Figure 7. Portrait of Christ in a building in Ostia.

Figure 8. Icon of the Virgin Mary in the church of Santa Francesca Romana.

Figure 9. Bronze statute of Saint Peter. Rome, Saint Peter's Basilica.

Figure 10. The wall of graffiti and the niche with the bones of Peter in the Vatican basilica.

Figure 11. Ancient Christian epigraph in the Lateran Museum of Sacred Art.

Figure 12. Church of Our Lady of Peace at Yamoussoukro (Ivory Coast).

3

THE CHRISTIAN "PRIMACIES" OF
THE CHURCH OF ROME

Besides the Catholic Church of Rome there are at the present time other Christian Churches, the product of the schisms of which I have already spoken: the Orthodox Church and the Reformed Church.

The Christian "primacies" (I insist on the quotation marks) of which I am about to speak are prerogatives of which only the Church of Rome can still boast today and which, taken together, undeniably lead one to reflect. Because much of the information concerning the individual topics has until now appeared only in the studies of specialists, I maintain that it is not inappropriate to speak here of the "primacies" with a certain amplitude so as to give for each of them as precise an idea as possible.

1. THE OLDEST "OFFICIAL" CHRISTIAN BASILICA:
THE LATERAN BASILICA

One of the "primacies" that the Church of Rome can boast about is that of possessing the oldest Christian basilica recognized as such by the civil authorities as well, which, in fact, carried out the plans for it from start to finish. I mean the Lateran basilica (figure 3). It is linked, as everyone knows, with the name of the emperor Constantine and with the memory of the fateful victory won by him on October 28 in

A.D. 312 at the gates of Rome, near the Milvian Bridge, over his rival Maxentius, son of Maximian.

It is well known that Christian worship took place at first in the intimacy of family households, in the *domus ecclesiae*, and that then, at one time or another, the need was felt to have suitable buildings in which the faithful could express their religious beliefs more freely and fully. Buildings of this sort must have sprung up rather quickly, probably as early as the third century, in the intervals, of course, between the various persecutions that the Christians had to undergo. The information that has come down to us, about these most ancient buildings, concerns above all the Christian East, which numbered large communities of believers led by bishops who were generally active and often wealthy, too. It was these bishops, encouraged naturally by the piety of the faithful and supported by their more or less generous offerings, who usually took the initiative of erecting the most ancient churches.

Very instructive in this regard is what we read in Eusebius, bishop of Caesarea, in the tenth and final book of his renowned *Ecclesiastical History*.[1] The book opens with a long panegyric of Paulinus, bishop of Tyre in Phoenicia, to whom the author is so kind as to dedicate his entire work. Paulinus, among his other accomplishments, constructed in Tyre, upon the ruins of an older church, a new temple (νεώς) that was larger and more splendid, which Eusebius does not hesitate to call the most beautiful in all Phoenicia. Before pausing to describe at length and in minute detail the new "House of Christ" (οἶκος Χριστοῦ), Eusebius speaks in general about the other churches that—in those days—had risen again, larger and more beautiful than before, from the ruins to which the tyrants had re-

---

[1] Eusebius, *Historia Ecclesiastica* 1–4. For the existence of the oldest churches, which had been destroyed and then restored, see 10, 2–3; for that of Tyre in particular, 10, 4, 1.

duced them out of hostility to the Christians. His words transport us to a period of religious peace in which, persecutions having ceased, two emperors showed the proper benevolence toward the Christians with documents (γϱάμματα), the conferral of honors (τιμαί), and generous gifts of money (χϱημάτων δόσεις). Since the two emperors in question are Constantine and Licinius, it can be determined that this period of religious peace and of enthusiastic construction fell between A.D. 315 and 319, as far as the Christian East is concerned. In reality, in 315 the two *Augusti*, after having defeated their rival Maximinus (313) and then fought among themselves (314), were reconciled and, to demonstrate the agreement that they had reached, took over the consulate together (315). On the other hand, in 319 Licinius, emperor of the East, started to display enmity toward the Christians, commanding among other things the closing of their churches. The panegyric of Eusebius, which presupposes the reconstruction of the churches in general and of the church in Tyre in particular, can therefore be dated around 318. However that may be, it is clear from the text of Eusebius that in Asia there was no lack of buildings set aside for Christian worship—buildings even older than the Lateran basilica. There were very probably others in Egypt and perhaps elsewhere.

But a little reflection shows that between these buildings and the Lateran basilica there is an essential difference. Whereas they were constructed at the initiative of zealous bishops and seconded morally and sometimes also materially by their respective faith communities, the Lateran basilica was erected at the command of the supreme civil authority of the emperor and, naturally, at his expense as well. Indeed, Constantine did not limit himself, in this case, to simple donations of money (χϱημάτων δόσεις), as happened in Asia, according to Eusebius, but rather took upon himself the entire cost of the project.

The Lateran basilica was consequently the first Christian building officially recognized as such: a prerogative proved both by the very name of *basilica*, an official term in itself, which was attributed to it from the very beginning, and also by the extraordinary magnificence with which the emperor wanted to adorn it, as we shall see. This prerogative was then joined by another, namely, that of being the sole Christian basilica that, after so many centuries and so many vicissitudes, still remains intact and in use, although with the inevitable modifications.

The existence of a building officially appointed for Christian worship in a city of the empire presupposes a contact, or even a close understanding, between the civil authority, represented by the emperor, and the religious authority, represented by the Christian Church, and this understanding came about for the first time in Rome, in 312, to be precise, after the victory of Constantine over Maxentius.

For the sake of accuracy, I wish to recall that, even before Constantine, another emperor, as it seems, had had the intention of constructing a building set aside for the religion of Christ. In fact, according to the *Historia Augusta*, already in the first half of the third century the emperor Severus Alexander (222–235), among other signs of an interest in Christianity, had proposed building a temple in honor of Christ, whom he considered worthy of being enumerated among the gods, but then he had dismissed the idea, warned by an oracle that, in any place where such a temple were to exist, everyone would become Christian and the temples of the other gods would be abandoned.[2]

---

[2] *Historia Augusta*, Alexander Severus, 43, 6f. For the interest of Severus Alexander in Christianity, see below, p. 85. Although the report about the pious intention of Severus Alexander is not improbable, many puzzling questions

Having duly recalled the pious intention of Severus Alexander, we should return to the concrete decision of Constantine and review briefly, in this regard, the events that preceded his famous and prophetic victory by the Milvian Bridge.

On the first of May in A.D. 305, Diocletian and Maximian, the two *Augusti* [or senior emperors, one in the East and one in the West], who in their day had divided the empire between them, laid down the supreme imperial authority. The initiative had been taken by Diocletian, the emperor of the East, who essentially held the highest authority, and Maximian had been obliged to follow his example, albeit reluctantly.

After the two abdications, which took place respectively in Nicomedia in Bithynia and in Milan, the power should have been transferred peacefully to the two *Caesars* [or junior emperors], Galerius in the East and Constantius Chlorus in the West. But things did not go that smoothly. The fact is that at one moment there were as many as six *Augusti* on the battlefield: three in the East and three in the West. In the Western empire, which is our main interest here, Constantius Chlorus very soon met his death (306), and immediately afterward the authority of his son Constantine asserted itself. In 307 Constantine married Fausta, the youngest daughter of Maximian, but family ties did not prevent him from clearing out of the way, one after the other, his father-in-law, Maximian, and his brother-in-law, Maxentius, who had become his rivals in the race for supreme power. Maximian,

---

still remain concerning that interpolation by the author of the *Vita* (which is attributed to Elius Lampridius) [to the effect] that even before Severus Alexander, the emperor Hadrian had had temples without statues erected, with the intention of including Christ also in that anonymity.

imprisoned, was forced to commit suicide (309), and against Maxentius, who was in Italy, Constantine took up arms for the decisive encounter. As you know, the arrival of the twenty-eighth of October in the year 312 marked the definitive victory of Constantine. The "usurper" Maxentius fell on the battlefield, and on the following day Constantine entered Rome in triumph. It was the first time he set foot in the city.

In Rome, the victorious young sovereign found that he was confronted by two different and contrasting authorities: the civil authority of the senate, which was still tenaciously bound to the traditions of the forefathers and generally was still devoted to the deities and rituals of paganism, and, on the other hand, the spiritual authority of a new religion—Christianity—which was already organized in a definite way and which repeated and severe persecutions had not succeeded in bringing down. Constantine, being an intelligent man, endowed with a cunning political sense, did not fail to perceive the vital force of the Christian Church, reaching out for the future, and he preferred to consider himself on Christ's side. Then again, he could not have been unaware of the fact that the Church of Rome was universally held to be the first, the most authoritative. In short, she possessed, as is once more evident, that spiritual primacy which all the other Christian communities have acknowledged her to have ever since the beginnings of Christianity. On the other hand, the Church of Rome did not overlook the importance of the spiritual and material advantages that would result from an agreement with the imperial authority. There was, then, a mutual attraction of the empire to the Church and of the Church to the empire.

Practically speaking, Constantine made it his duty to confer honors and benefices upon the Christians, beginning precisely with that Church of Rome which was the most important of all. So it happened that, in that very moment, the pomp and splendor that until then had been foreign to her burst in upon the Church of Rome. In such an atmosphere arose the first Christian basilica in Rome.

The decision to erect in the city a great building dedicated to Christian worship was certainly made by Constantine immediately after his victory over Maxentius. He determined also to consecrate it to that same Christ the Savior who had obviously shown that he would help him in his undertaking. It should be recalled, in this connection, that the victory by the Milvian Bridge was surrounded, at a certain moment, by a prodigious halo, a large part of which consisted of a miraculous sign of Christ, oscillating between the initials of his divine name and the Cross on which he died: ✗, ✝, ☧.

It is helpful to note also that, even though the tradition about the marvel was enlarged upon and embellished later on by the same Constantine, it is undeniable that on the very day after the battle there was talk in Rome of a miraculous and mysterious intervention of Christ.[3]

As for Christ the Savior and the importance that Constantine attributed to his protection, I will not fail to mention that the figure of Christ, who had favored his success, was predominant in the long run, from then on, in the emperor's thinking. More than ten years later he still thought of Christ and of him alone when, in 324, after conquering his rival Licinius in the battle of Chrysopolis and becoming the sole sovereign of the immense empire, he decided to establish the capital thereof in Byzantium and to give it his own

---

[3] On this topic, cf. my essay, "Le acclamazioni a Cristo e alla Croce e la visione di Costantino", in *Mélanges ... offerts à Pierre Boyancé*, Collection de l'École Française de Rome, 22 (Rome, 1974), pp. 370–86.

name (Constantinople). To which heavenly patron did he want to entrust it? According to a very widespread opinion, he would have entrusted it to the Blessed Virgin. But that is not exactly true. In reality, the patronage of the Blessed Virgin began to take shape only in the sixth century, to be affirmed decisively then in the seventh. Originally the city was entrusted, to be precise, to Christ, and the two oldest Christian churches of Constantinople, *Hagía Eirene* and *Hagía Sophia*,[4] took their names specifically from two of his attributes (peace and wisdom).

We return now to Rome. It is extremely probable (I repeat) that the decision to erect a great basilica as a votive offering to Christ the Savior was undertaken by the emperor immediately after his victory over Maxentius. The site selected for the construction—the neighborhood of the Lateran—suggests, in turn, a certain amount of reflection. When Constantine entered Rome, that neighborhood, once possessed by the eminent family of the *Laterani*, belonged to the imperial patrimony. Here, in the immediate vicinity of the city walls, was located the sumptuous villa in which Maximian had lived with his family. The grandiose ruins discovered along what is today the Via Amba Aradam were part of this regal dwelling, in which Fausta was born, from whom it later took the name of Domus Faustae. Everything leads us to believe that, as soon as Constantine entered Rome, he did not go to live in the imperial palace of the Palatine (he went there only on the occasion of his second sojourn, in 315), but rather took up residence in the house of the Lateran, which had become the property of his wife, Fausta, by inheritance. Later, in late Janu-

---

[4] Cf. G. Dagron, *Naissance d'une capitale: Constantinople et ses institutions de 330 à 451* (Paris, 1974), pp. 38f., 42, 386f.

ary 313, when he left Rome to rejoin his Eastern colleague Licinius, who was awaiting him in Milan, it was his good pleasure to leave the Domus Faustae to Pope Miltiades, who on October 2 of the same year opened there, with the explicit consent of the emperor, the council that was to settle the schism of the Donatists.[5]

If, then, the Lateran belonged to Constantine and he wanted to offer to the popes their first permanent and dignified residence there—even, as it seems, in the very house where he had lived—it is not strange that the far-sighted sovereign should want to have the great basilica dedicated to Christ the Savior built at the same location. The new edifice would have to be, in reality, very near to the Domus Faustae, in a place already occupied by the barracks of the equestrian guard (*equites singulares*), with an annexed administrative building, which at a later date became the Patriarchio.

Now one might ask when, more precisely, the Lateran basilica was constructed. An ancient tradition claims that the basilica was dedicated on the ninth of November.[6] Since the dedication of sacred buildings, among the Christians, usually occurred on a Sunday, considering the reign of Constantine and of Pope Sylvester, who succeeded Miltiades

[5] For the Domus Faustae and its assignment by Constantine to Pope Miltiades, cf. another essay of mine: "La *Domus Faustae* in Laterano e la Cattedra di san Pietro in Vaticano", in *Studien . . . Friedrich Wilhelm Deichmann gewidmet* (Mainz, 1986), pp. 249–63; illustrations, 59–61. I report there some quotations of particular interest with regard to the birth of Fausta in Rome; Julian, *Orat.* 14. For the Domus Faustae as the site of the council that would invalidate the schism of the Donatists: Optatus of Milevis, 1, 23, Corpus scriptorum Ecclesiasticorum Latinorum, vol. 36, p. 26). For the interests of Constantine in the council with regard to the aforementioned schism: Eusebius, *Historia* 10, 5, 18–20; Optatus of Milevis, 1, 22, Corpus scriptorum Eccl. Latinorum vol. 26, pp. 25–27.

[6] Cf. C. Baronio, *Martyrologium Romanum* (Venice, 1597), p. 505.

(in 314), and during whose pontificate the basilica was in large part constructed, we have a choice between November 9, 312, and November 9, 318. It is a practical impossibility for the dedication to have taken place on November 9, 312, that is, around ten days after the battle by the Milvian Bridge. The date falls, then, in 318, and this time the calculations come out right. If Constantine, as everything leads us to believe, decided upon the erection of the basilica before his departure from Rome (late January of the year 313), the basilica could have been ready for the solemn dedication by November 9, 318. Its construction and furnishing would have required around six years: a period that is well in keeping with what we know about the duration of construction projects of an official sort during the empire. Therefore, if the basilica really was dedicated on November 9, 318, it is interesting to note that the church in Tyre that was extolled by Eusebius was probably dedicated around that same year, as we have seen, though of course in quite different circumstances.

Annexed to the basilica, at the emperor's command, arose its respective baptistery, and this of course had as its patron John the Baptist, the saint from whom Christ himself had received baptism (figure 4). We have reason to believe that the noblest sacred edifices that the pagan religion had raised up from the ground of the city served as models for both of these Christian buildings. Basilica and baptistery were then decorated, sparing no expense, with a magnificence that was entirely in keeping with that of the imperial residence (the Domus Faustae), in which, in accordance with Constantine's will, Pope Miltiades and after him his successor, Sylvester, had come to live. Both the basilica and the baptistery must have been, inside, a shining display of rare marbles (figure 5), a resplendent collection of precious metals and gems, lit by lamps that had been sagaciously positioned. Some idea of such great splendor is given by the *Liber Pontificalis* [Pontifical book] in the *Vita* of Pope Sylvester, a *Vita* that was composed at the beginning of the sixth century, not without reference to older sources, some of which could have gone back to the fourth century. It should be noted that the author of the *Vita* still attributes to the basilica the name of *Constantiniana*, in memory of its imperial founder.[7]

The generous emperor had then wanted to endow basilica and baptistery with a considerable yearly income. These funds were derived from landed properties situated for the most part in the vicinity of Rome, but also in distant localities in Africa and in Greece. Properties situated in Asia did not yet figure in the endowment, because it was only after 324, when his rival Licinius, the emperor of the East, was defeated in the battle of Chrysopolis, that Constantine, the sole remaining sovereign, could dispose of Asian lands as well. To the basilica was assigned, in all, an annual income of 4,390 solidi, to the baptistery an income of 10,234 solidi. These were big numbers: a veritable rain of gold. But why, we might ask, was the income set for the baptistery so much more substantial than that destined for the basilica? The answer is easy when one considers that that stupendous sum had to include also the endowment of the one who at that time had the exclusive right of administering, precisely in that building, the sacrament of baptism: I mean the pope. This splendid

---

[7] *Liber Pontificalis*, ed. L. Duchesne, 1:272–74. Of particular interest, in the description of such beauteous splendor, is the mention of the [semi-circular] hollow of the apse (*camera*), clothed in precious gold brocade. On this subject, cf. my observations in the essay entitled "Camerae fulgentes" in *Studi in onore di Ettore Paratore* (Rome, 1981), 2:799–817. Pages 803ff. refer to the *camera fulgens* [resplendent chamber] of the Lateran basilica.

"stipend" was in keeping, furthermore, with the magnificence in which the Church had begun to clothe herself.

In the second half of the twelfth century the basilica was still named after Christ the Savior,[8] but later it permanently assumed the name of San Giovanni from the two oratories annexed to the baptistery: the one born of the original cult of Saint John the Baptist and the subsequent one dedicated to the other Giovanni, that is, to Saint John the Evangelist. Let it be noted that the name of Saint John began to be extended, though not uninterruptedly, to the basilica as well from the time of Gregory the Great (590–604). After the period of the exile in Avignon (1305–1377) and of the Great Schism (1378–1417), during which the popes were almost always absent from Rome, the pontiffs who returned definitively abandoned their ancient residence in the Lateran, but the Lateran basilica always remained the cathedral of Rome and the title of "archibasilica" always belonged to it alone.

Finally, in order to prove the importance of the most ancient "official" basilica that Rome can boast of possessing, I would like to direct your attention to certain epithets that are applied to it in a *Descriptio Lateranensis Ecclesiae* composed during the pontificate of Alexander III (1159–1181) by Giovanni the Deacon, based on older versions dating back to the second half of the preceding eleventh century.[9] In that ancient description the basilica was named, among other things, *Aurea* [golden] for its great splendor, *sedes prima* [primal see] for its priority with respect to the sees of Antioch (second) and of Alexandria (third), *sedes Romanae ecclesiae* [seat of the Roman church] from the city of Rome in which it is

[8] Cf. the description of the basilica in R. Valentini, G. Zucchetti, *Codice topografico della città di Roma*, vol. 3 (Rome, 1946), pp. 334f.
[9] Ibid.

preeminent, *Universalis ecclesia* [universal church], because of the ecumenical authority of the bishop who resided there. But particularly significant and eloquent in themselves are the epithets of *Caput ecclesiarum* [Head of the churches], *Mater ecclesiarum* [Mother of churches], *Magistra ecclesiarum* [Teacher of churches], "because all receive from her their impetus and their teaching authority".

Centuries have passed since the time of Giovanni the Deacon, but the basilica of the "primacy" is still called today *Papalis sacrosancta Archibasilica Lateranensis Cathedralis Romae* [the most sacred papal cathedral-archibasilica at the Lateran in Rome].

2. THE OLDEST PORTRAIT OF CHRIST

We do not know what the physical appearance of Christ was like, and our ignorance in this matter is, I should say, inevitable. In fact it is not clear how a reliable image of Jesus could have come down to us, when we consider that Jesus was born, lived, and died in Palestine and that in Palestine the artistic representation of a human being would have been, at least in principle, an act of idolatry. The same reasoning is valid for the first generation of Christians; since almost all of them were of Jewish descent, the idea of a portrait must have been quite foreign to them as well.

With the spread of Christianity, however, the proselytes, growing more and more numerous and belonging to an ever greater variety of peoples, felt more and more strongly the impulse to behold in its concrete form the ineffable face of the God-Man. But how should it be imagined? In this connection two different trends began to manifest themselves, both of them suggested by the Old Testament. On the one hand, the prophetic vision of Isaiah evoked the Christ of the

Passion, ugly, emaciated, and suffering;[10] on the other hand, Psalm 45 presented a Messiah resplendent with grace and beauty.[11]

At a certain moment the idea of beauty prevailed, and Jesus became an example of physical perfection, in every detail of his body. So he was described, for example, in the ninth century by Epiphanius, bishop of Constantinople:[12] a description that made its way to the West and became widespread there. It was natural, then, that Christ, imagined as handsome, should be presented now as an beardless youth, now as an adult man well endowed with a beard and mustache. Given this situation, I want to specify that, in speaking about a "portrait of Christ", I have in mind here not a Christ-figure accompanied by other figures and therefore set in a narrative context, and not even the Christ of the well-known motif of the *traditio legis*; I am thinking instead of an image of the Redeemer executed with the primary purpose of rendering his features, that is, precisely, of making a portrait of him.

Well, the oldest mention of a portrait of Christ brings us to Rome, and once more at Rome we are fortunate enough to find the oldest portrait of Christ that has come down to our day. Many documents, it is true, have been lost, and, as for the works of art themselves, it cannot be denied that in the Christian East, the battle against the veneration of images (iconoclasm) raged for more than a century (726–843), during which many sacred images were ruthlessly destroyed, and it is logical to admit that among the others, even before the others, many images of Christ were targeted, whether

[10] Is 53:2.
[11] Ps 45:3.
[12] Epiphanius, *De vita beatae Virginis*, in *Patrologia Graeca*, 120, 204.

they were contemporary or of older origin. The fact remains, however, that *today*, in order to find the oldest information about portraits of Christ and, concretely, his oldest portrait, we must once again return to Rome.

The oldest notices about portraits of Christ

In the Greek East, the oldest mention of portraits of Christ goes back to the first half of the fourth century. In his *Ecclesiastical History*, which was concluded in the year 324 after the victory of Constantine over his rival Licinius, Eusebius, bishop of Caesarea, speaks of a bronze statue of Christ existing at Caesarea Philippi (the Phoenician city of Paneas) near the source of the Jordan River. In this city, the hometown of the woman with the hemorrhage who was cured by Christ, and right in front of the door of her house, the aforementioned statue of the Savior is said to have stood. Facing it, another bronze statue represented the woman, on her knees, about to receive the grace of healing.[13] But it is anything but certain that Jesus could really be recognized in the first of the two statues, and many in fact have doubted it. There is no doubt, however, about what Eusebius adds a little farther on: that he himself had seen in Palestine images (εἰϰόνες) of Peter, of Paul, and of Christ himself "preserved on wooden tablets".[14] This is, as yet, the first record that has come down to us of portraits of Christ in the Christian world of the East.

In the Christian world of the West, however, the records go back even farther.

While speaking of the power of attraction that Rome and its Church exercised in the second century on Christians

---

[13] Eusebius, *Historia* 7, 18, 1–3.
[14] Ibid., 18, 4.

and even on heretics from all parts of the empire, I recalled that at the time of Pope Anicetus (155–166) a certain Marcellina came to Rome and probably remained there; she was a determined supporter of the heretical movement promoted by the Egyptian Carpocrates.[15] The information is found in a passage of that great work against heresies which was written in the second half of that same second century, that is, not many years after Anicetus, by Irenaeus, bishop of Lyons.[16] After mentioning the arrival of Marcellina in Rome and the active propaganda that she carried on in favor of her sect, Irenaeus adds, with regard to the Carpocratian heretics, an interesting note: "They have certain images depicted or executed in another material, and they say that the model of Christ (*forma Christi*) was made by Pilate during the time in which Jesus lived among men." Later on this singular note is taken up again, in a somewhat retouched form, by other authors. It will suffice to recall here the words that Augustine wrote at the beginning of the fifth century in his work on heresies: "The Carpocratians are so called from Carpocrates. According to a tradition of the same sect, there was a certain Marcellina, who venerated images of Jesus and of Paul and of Homer and of Pythagoras, honoring them and incensing them." [17]

Naturally we have every right to call into question what Irenaeus relates concerning a true "likeness" of Jesus executed or ordered to be executed by none other than Pilate! It seems undeniable, however, that during the second century, in Carpocratian circles, small pictures or statuettes or

---

[15] See above, pp. 15–16.

[16] Irenaeus, *Adversus haereses* 1, 25, 6. On this passage, compare the observations of P. Corby Finney, in *Rivista di archeologia cristiana* 57 (1981): 35–41.

[17] Augustine, *De haeresibus* 7.

other artworks were common, in which the followers of Carpocrates recognized a typical image of Christ, and because Irenaeus speaks of Marcellina and of her coming to Rome and of her propaganda activity, it follows that we have reports especially in Rome of these images, albeit heretical, of Jesus.

Still at Rome we find the mention of another ancient portrait of Christ: a portrait that takes us from the heretical circle of the zealot Marcellina into the rather different ambiance of the imperial court. I am alluding to the portrait, or presumed portrait, of Christ that was honored in the *lararium* [or chapel dedicated to the *Lares*, tutelary deities of the Romans] of Severus Alexander (222–235). In the *Vita* of this emperor, the *Historia Augusta* relates that in his *lararium* on the Palatine were found portraits (*effigies*) of divinized sovereigns, of his own ancestors, and of other men who were considered to be among the elect, such as the famous thaumaturge [wonder-worker] Apollonius of Tiana, Christ, Abraham, and Orpheus. The emperor would render homage to these images whenever he could, in the morning hours.[18] The *Vita* of Severus Alexander, attributed to Aelius Lampridius, was written in the fourth century or at the beginning of the fifth, but there is no doubt that in writing it the author had used older sources.[19]

The association of the images of Christ, of Abraham, of Orpheus, not to mention of Apollonius of Tiana, vividly calls to mind the association that the heretic Marcellina, as

---

[18] *Historia Augusta*, Alexander Severus, 29, 2.

[19] The author himself attests that he obtained the information about the portraits of Christ, Abraham, and Orpheus from a contemporary *scriptor* of the emperor. It is difficult to assign a name to him, but it is still permissible to believe that the name really was present in the memory of the author himself.

we have seen, had established in the preceding century among the images of Christ, Paul, Homer, and Pythagoras—images that she held to be equally worthy of her veneration and of her incense. In both cases we are dealing with religious eclecticism, which however is manifested at very different levels. Onto the devotion of Marcellina and the Carpocratians is grafted, to be sure, a bit of superstition, accompanied perhaps by a certain dose of fanaticism; Severus Alexander, on the other hand, an intelligent and educated man, seems to have wanted to gather in his *lararium* a well-planned *florilegium*, or gallery of images of men (among whom is included also the mythical Orpheus) who, thanks to their exceptional virtue, had entered into the sphere of divinity. In that company of great spirits was found, then, in the emperor's judgment, Jesus Christ.

Meditating on that page from the *Historia Augusta*, one author, not erroneously, has given prominence to the religious eclecticism of Severus Alexander.[20] And yet it is permissible to observe, I believe, that, as far as the portrait of Christ is concerned, something more was evidently joined to the eclecticism. Indeed, it cannot be overlooked that the Roman emperor had had a genuine interest in the extraordinary figure of Jesus and in Christianity generally. The same *Historia Augusta* furnishes us with eloquent proofs of this: both the note, of which I have already spoken, about the ruler's intention to erect a Christian church[21] and also other indications that are no less significant.[22] Besides, the pro-

---

[20] See, for example, S. Settis, "Severo Alessandro e i suoi lari", in *Aevum* 60 (1972): 237–51.

[21] See above, p. 72.

[22] *Historia Augusta* 45, 6f.; 51, 7f. Cf. E. dal Convolo, *I Severi e il Cristianesimo* (Rome, 1989), pp. 77ff.

Christian attitude of Severus Alexander finds corroboration in the interest shown by his mother, the intelligent and well-educated Julia Mamea, toward the spiritual movements of that era and, in particular, toward Christianity. Not insignificantly, during one of her sojourns in Antioch she requested instruction concerning the truths of the Christian faith from the learned Origen.[23] However that may be, the *lararium* of Severus Alexander on the Palatine contained—during the first half of the third century—an eminent portrait of Christ (or what was believed to be one). But where could it have come from?

It is difficult to believe that the sophisticated emperor had exhibited and venerated in his royal palace one of the "Pilatesque" images of Christ that the heretical devotion of Marcellina and her companions in faith had introduced in Rome in the preceding century. The portrait of Jesus honored by the emperor seems to have had different origins. I believe that I am not far from the truth in thinking that Julius Africanus may have played a part in this. This man was, as everyone knows, the very learned Christian who had gained the confidence of the emperor, to whom he had dedicated his encyclopedic work entitled *Kestoi* (*Embroideries*) and who at his command had organized the beautiful library of the Pantheon near the [Thermal] Baths of Agrippa, which were then called the Alexandrine Baths after the current ruler. A Palestinian by birth, Julius Africanus had close ties to the court of Edessa in Mesopotamia, a city that by that time had become an ardent center of Judaeo-Christian life.

For a Palestinian Christian in contact with Edessa it must not have been difficult to procure for the emperor an image

---

[23] Eusebius, *Historia* 6, 2, 3; Jerome, *De viris illustribus* 54.

of that extraordinary man who had made so many disciples throughout the empire and in Rome itself, of that Christ who was so fascinating that not even the empress-mother was immune to it.

What this portrait looked like, then, is difficult to say precisely. But it seems probable that it was not so much a sculpture as a painting; one of those icons that in the following century Eusebius would see with his own eyes in the Palestinian region.

The oldest portrait of Christ that has come down to us

The oldest image of Christ executed with the intention of making a portrait is, as far as I know, the one that is found in the catacomb of Commodilla, the well-known Christian cemetery situated above a side road off the Via Ostiense.[24] Thus we are once again in Rome (figure 6).

The portrait of the Redeemer is painted as a fresco on the ceiling of the cubicle of Leo, an official who was responsible for the collection of taxes. This ceiling, originally conceived in the form of a cross, was adapted during the work on the image that the artist intended to apply to it. In the primitive design the ceiling was supposed to present a pattern of squares with red borders, each containing a yellow eight-pointed star. When it was decided to insert into the decorative pattern the exceptional ornament of a portrait of Christ, nine of the squares disappeared beneath a coat of white paint and the

---

[24] A. Ferrua, in *Rivista di archeologia cristiana* 34 (1958): 17–19, fig. 14. Less distinct qualities of a portrait are found in the image of Christ contained in a medallion in cubicle 4 of the catacomb of Domitilla (cf. J. Wilpert, *Le pitture delle catacombe romane* [Rome, 1903], plate 187, no. 3), which is perhaps a little older.

cruciform vault was smoothed so as to obtain a rectangle 66 cm. wide and 53 cm. high, destined to receive the portrait.

Christ is represented here with the features of an adult, with a beard and mustache, with long, wavy hair falling to his shoulders, and wearing a tunic and pallium. His head is surrounded by a blue nimbus [halo] edged in red and flanked by the apocalyptic letters *alpha* and *omega*. As for the age of the painting (and for us this takes on a special importance), it can be stated that various arguments of an archaeological and topographical character take us back to the years 375–380.

This portrait of Jesus is, as I said, the oldest one that is known thus far, but nobody would venture to say that in Rome there are not others even older or, to put it a better way, that there is not some older portrait that served as the model for this one that we are speaking of, or for others.

Before discussing the hypothetical model, however, I would like to pause and look at another interesting portrait of Christ, which is close to the one in the catacomb of Commodilla in age as well as in the place of its discovery. I am referring to the portrait of Christ executed in the technique of *opus sectile* [a sort of mosaic composed of larger custom-cut pieces] in an extant building in Ostia near the Porta Marina (figure 7).

The excavation of this building, initiated by the late Giovanni Becatti in June 1959, was elucidated by him in a volume published in 1969.[25] The aforementioned building, probably the site of a *collegium*, comprised among other things a great *aula* [hall], in the upper part of which are found Christian images. The age of the building was determined not only from the style of the illustrated decorations, but also from certain providential coins [found at the site]. One of

[25] G. Becatti, *Scavi di Ostia*, vol. 6: *Edificio con* opus sectile *presso Porta Marina* (Rome, 1969).

them, a little bronze piece left behind by chance in the mortar of the construction, bore the name of the emperor Maximus (385–388);[26] others, scattered here and there, were from a more recent era, but no later than 394. The Christian setting, which certainly does not predate 385, seems to have been interrupted at a certain moment and partially demolished. This happened probably in the final anti-Christian reaction of paganism, a reaction that had its epilogue precisely between the fifth and the sixth of September in the year 394, the date on which the troops of the emperor Theodosius defeated those of the usurper Eugenius in the battlefield by the river Frigido near Aquileia.

In the frieze executed in *opus sectile* that decorated the walls of the Christian *aula* appeared symbols alluding quite clearly to the religion of Christ. Becatti collected quite a lot of the fragments remaining from them.[27] Among other things, there was a gemmed cross, fish, doves, and also snails—the latter, as I myself found it explained elsewhere, were compared by Christians to souls, who carry their homes (that is, their bodies) with them ready to welcome the commands of Heaven, to reach then for the happiness of Paradise.[28] But what struck Becatti above all, and still strikes us today, is the extraordinary portrait of Christ on the right-hand wall.[29]

This portrait was deliberately placed in full view, in a central position with respect to the width and the height of the wall, as though within a metope [the space between two tablets of a Doric frieze] and flanked by two round shields.

---

[26] Cf. Becatti, *Edificio*, p. 41, plate 42, 1.

[27] Ibid., pp. 161–67, plates 73–74.

[28] Cf. M. Guarducci, *I graffiti sotto la Confessione di San Pietro in Vaticano* (Vatican City, 1958), 1:489–95, fig. 251.

[29] Becatti, *Edificio*, pp. 139–41, plates 55, 1–56.

The figure of Jesus, limited to a bust, stands out clearly against an inlaid background [*tarsia*] of red porphyry framed with bands of yellow Numidian marble. Let it be noted immediately that red porphyry is the royal stone, just as purple is the royal cloth. Here, then, the inlaid porphyry seems to be the equivalent of a precious purple drapery that serves as a background for the figure of Christ the King.

The Redeemer is depicted here with the features of an adult man, with a beard, mustache, and long wavy hair. The eyes are large, open, and almost staring, with the pupils strongly marked. Within the beard the red mouth stands out vividly. Jesus is clothed in a tunic and pallium of white material and has around his head a nimbus of similar whiteness. In keeping with the appearance of an adult man is the gesture of the upraised right hand. This is the sign of one who is teaching, with three fingers extended and two folded, a gesture that reveals Christ in his prerogative of Master of eternal life. It should be noted, then, that the bust is slightly turned to one side, as though to welcome those who cross the threshold of the noble setting, of which, clearly, he is considered the patron.

The building dates back, as I explained, to shortly after 385. This calls to mind a suggestive memory: namely, that precisely between 387 and 388 Saint Augustine, who had already been converted and baptized by Ambrose, had the occasion to live at Ostia, though not continuously. In the autumn of 387 he was there together with his mother, Monica, who eventually passed away right there in Ostia, and in 388 he returned to the city alone, to wait for a ship that would set sail for Africa, which happened after the death of the emperor Maximus (August 28, 388). Augustine found in Ostia the basilica that had been built there at Constantine's command in honor of the apostles Peter and Paul and of

John the Baptist, and he almost certainly found there as well already in progress the construction of the Christian building that interests us, though probably not yet enriched with all of its decoration.

Confronted with the ancient portrait of Christ in the cemetery of Commodilla, followed a short time later by the one in the building in Ostia, we are led spontaneously to wonder, by what model, certainly a Roman one, they could have been inspired.

I maintain that I am not too far from the truth in thinking that the model must be sought in the oldest "official" Christian basilica, that is, in the Lateran (or Constantinian) basilica, which the victorious emperor had his subjects erect in honor of Christ. A large image of the Savior, probably a mosaic, must once have adorned the interior of the building. But where, precisely?

A medieval legend, dating back to a time ranging between the tenth and eleventh century, speaks of an image of Christ that appeared miraculously in the apse of the basilica; and scholars have meditated and fantasized a bit on this subject.[30] The numerous changes that the building underwent over the centuries prevent us from determining whether the great image that inspired the legend actually existed in the apse. Nevertheless it is reasonable to assume that it was right there, and not in the vaulted ceiling, which, as I hope to have demonstrated, must originally have been covered with a heavy gold fabric, but rather in the arch of the apse, which would have lent itself well to receiving a portrait of supreme importance, such as that of Christ the Savior.

---

[30] On this subject cf. C. Cecchelli, *La Santa Sindone nelle ricerche moderne* (Turin, 1980), pp. 153–65.

3. THE OLDEST PORTRAIT OF MARY

After the portrait of Christ, the one of Mary.

A study that I wrote on this topic was recently published, the fruit of a long and complex investigation.[31] From those pages of mine I will relate here the principal facts, which (it should be made clear at the outset) lead to the same conclusion we arrived at with respect to Christ: namely, that in order to find the oldest portrait of Mary yet known, we must remain in Rome.

As with Christ, so also with Mary, I mean, in speaking of a "portrait", not an image incorporated into a narrative context, but rather an image executed with the purpose of reproducing the characteristic features of the personage who is represented. In referring to an image of this type, one could also use, as in Christ's case, the term "icon".

In Mary's case, too, it would be absurd to assume the existence of a prototype painted from life in Palestine. A widespread tradition both in the East and in the West claims that Luke, the third evangelist, had had the privilege of portraying from life the likeness of the Blessed Virgin. But this tradition, to which writers testify, as we shall see, for the first time in the sixth century, is naturally only a pious legend. Luke, a native of Antioch, was a physician. His transformation from physician to painter resulted, it appears, from the fact that the Gospel of Luke is centered upon the figure of Mary and is the only one to contain episodes dealing with the infancy of Jesus; perhaps it was prompted also by the intention that Luke himself expresses at the beginning

---

[31] M. Guarducci, *La più antica icone di Maria; un prodigioso vincolo fra Oriente e Occidente* (Rome, 1988). See also my brief article in *Augustinianum* 30 (1990): 484–87.

of his Gospel to adhere scrupulously to the reports of eyewitnesses.

Between the end of the fourth century and the first years of the fifth, Saint Augustine wrote in one his treatises (and I quote him verbatim): "We do not know the face of the Virgin Mary";[32] and essentially he was right. Nevertheless Christians had not given up and subsequently would not give up imagining and contemplating that face with the eyes of the mind, especially in those places where the cult of the Virgin had manifested itself early on. Thus, it is permissible to postulate already in the fourth century the presence of Marian images in Egypt, in Palestine, in Asia Minor, even though not one of these images has come down to us. The presence of "portraits" of Mary becomes the norm, I could almost say by necessity, after 431. In that year at Ephesus, as everyone knows, the council took place that solemnly proclaimed the divine maternity of Mary, and it is logical that this provided an incentive for the cult of the Virgin Mother of God (Θεοτόκος) and produced a demand for her images. While the great basilica of Santa Maria Maggiore [Saint Mary Major] was arising in splendor at Rome, in Constantinople—especially at the initiative of Pulcheria, the pious sister of the emperor Theodosius II—provisions were being made to erect three churches, and in the most important one, that of the *Hodigói*, they were thinking of placing a large image of Mary, which appropriately had been brought from the Holy Land.

A Byzantine writer who lived in Constantinople in the sixth century, Theodore the Lector, has handed down to us the story that "Eudocia sent to Pulcheria from Jerusalem the

---

[32] Augustine, *De Trinitate* 8, 5 (*Patrologia Latina*, 42, 952).

image of the Mother of God that the evangelist Luke had painted."[33] Eudocia was the reigning empress, wife of Theodosius II and sister-in-law of Pulcheria; she was traveling on pilgrimage in Palestine in order to fulfill a vow that she had made some years previously.

Some have raised doubts about this information from Theodore the Lector; not only about the tradition concerning Luke, but also about Eudocia sending the Marian icon. Still, although the tradition concerning Luke is really only a legend, there are no good reasons to deny the gift of the icon. Instead, let it be noted that, according to our source, Eudocia "sent" the image of the Virgin. Since it is known with certainty that in 439 she made her return to Constantinople, the shipment means that the image arrived at its destination before the empress returned, that is, in 438, while she was still in Palestine, intent on visiting the holy places. It is likewise clear that, in Constantinople, Pulcheria was in something of a hurry to obtain the precious icon "of Luke". In any event it is certain that we are dealing with the image intended for the church of the *Hodigói*, which at that time must have been finished or almost completed.

The icon of Mary arrived, then, in the capital of the empire and was solemnly enshrined in the church of the *Hodigói*, where the Virgin acquired the name of *Hodigítria*. From other sources we learn that the image was painted in encaustic on a large, heavy slab of wood. Actually there is reason to think (and this will be confirmed by circumstances I will mention farther on) that the icon sent by Eudocia to Pulcheria consisted of a circular piece of wood containing only the head of the Madonna, painted larger than life; that is to

[33] Theodore the Lector, *Historia Ecclesiastica* 1, 5 (*Patrologia Graeca*, 85, 165).

say, that it had been one of those *imagines clipeatae* [disk- or shield-shaped images] that enjoyed great popularity during the imperial era. At Constantinople the precious circle seems to have been entrusted to skilled local artists, who inserted it into the large, heavy slab and added the rest of the picture, including the Child—complying, of course, with the encaustic technique and the larger-than-life dimensions of the original that the head of the Virgin suggested.

Be that as it may, it is certain that the great icon, the *Hodigítria*, enriched and sanctified by the "portrait" of the Madonna that "Luke" had painted, was for long centuries the object of an intense devotion, as the patroness of the empire and of the people. Adorned with superb jewels, the icon was, at Constantinople, the centerpiece of characteristic rituals and unceasingly drew throngs of believers, not only from every part of the empire, but even from more distant lands, such as Russia, Egypt, and the Iberian Peninsula.

After participating for so many centuries in the life of the empire, the most venerable *Hodigítria* also witnessed its fall and was a victim thereof. In 1453, after Constantinople had fallen into the hands of the Turks, the great icon suffered indeed the supreme insult. Impious Janissaries took possession of the superb jewels that adorned it, shattered it with axe blows, and threw the sacred fragments into the waters of the Bosphorus.

As long as the Madonna was exposed to the veneration of the faithful, it gave rise to numerous imitations, which vary in quite a few of their details. But what did the authentic face of the famous icon really look like? Since it perished in the waters of the Bosphorus, it seemed that all hope of knowing the true features of the *Hodigítria* was lost. But it was not so. Thanks to an extraordinary concatenation of events, the face of the Virgin had been saved.

After five centuries it was almost miraculously discovered, at Rome, to be precise, and it is to this day the most ancient portrait of the Virgin that has come down to us.

On the eve of the Holy Year 1950, when the churches of Rome were seeking to gather and, where necessary, to restore their respective treasures so as to exhibit them to the piety and the admiration of future pilgrims, the church of Santa Francesca Romana near the Forum also devoted particular care to an ancient icon that represented the Virgin with the Child on her arm (figure 8). The icon, which had long been venerated, had undergone more or less successful restorations, the last of which dated back to 1805. Now, it was entrusted to the expert art restorer Pico Cellini.

The restoration brought to light from beneath the faces of the Madonna and the Child two other older faces painted in tempera on canvas, which seemed to date from the thirteenth century. But at a deeper level there were yet two more faces, larger and much older. These were painted in encaustic (that is, with colors dissolved in liquid wax) on linen cloth and, as was later proved, had been cut from an enormous image on fabric and applied to a tablet of oriental wood. This image was certainly the original, upon which the restorations from the 1300s and 1800s had been superimposed.

The face of the Virgin, still practically intact, had a pale coloring. The eyes were large, dark, and slightly melancholy; the nose was straight and pointed; the mouth, small and vividly rose-colored. The head, surrounded by a veil or, rather, enclosed within a sort of cap (*maphórion*) of a bright blue color enlivened with streaks of azure, was covered by a mantle of a somber color between azure and violet. The face of the Child that emerged was somewhat damaged. It was possible, though, to distinguish around his neck the red collar of a little white tunic on which (this will be examined later on) a little pallium had been thrown. Both heads were surrounded by a halo, and in that of the Child could be distinguished the traces of an inscribed cross.

The restorer recognized in this ancient image an Egyptian style, dated it to the fifth century, and determined that it had a connection with the church of Santa Maria Antiqua [Old Saint Mary's], located at the foot of the northern slope of the Palatine Hill, a church that eventually had as its heir Santa Maria Nova [New Saint Mary's], which was then called Santa Francesca Romana [Saint Frances of Rome].[34]

The discovery of this extremely old image caused a great commotion, which lasted for quite a long time. But the judgments expressed by scholars (and there were many of them) about the mysterious Madonna were certainly not unanimous; so much so that the proposed dates ranged between the fifth and the eleventh centuries!

Such was the state of affairs when I began my work. Proceeding according to methods that were, I should say, strictly rigorous and calling upon the findings of various academic disciplines, I arrived at a sensational result, which I will summarize briefly here.

The ancient image painted in encaustic is the mirror image, executed upon a direct imprint, of the famous *Hodigítria* of Constantinople. The fact that we are dealing here with an imprint is confirmed, among other ways, by the unusual position of the Child on the Virgin's right arm instead of on her left.

The copy was made in Constantinople between 438 and 439, shortly after the arrival of the icon from Palestine, and

---

[34] P. Cellini, in *Proporzioni* 3 (1950): 1–8, plates 1–11. This issue of the review was dedicated to Pietro Toesca. The article had the title "Una Madonna molto antica".

was sent to the sovereigns of the Western empire, Valentinian III and Licinia Eudoxia, respectively the son-in-law and daughter of the sovereigns of the Eastern empire.

The sovereigns of the Western empire received the precious copy at Ravenna, their customary residence, probably during the summer of 439, but almost immediately—in autumn of the same year—they brought it to Rome, to the Palatine, where they stayed until late spring of the year 440.

It should be noted that in that era the cult of Mary was flourishing magnificently in Rome, where Pope Sixtus III was completing the construction and the decoration of the basilica of Santa Maria Maggiore.

The icon remained on the Palatine Hill for some time, at least until the middle of the fifth century; then, with the decline of the Western empire, and hence of the royal palace of the Palatine, it was transferred to the nearby church of Santa Maria Antiqua, where it made its way—after being renovated—into the church of Santa Maria Nova, which was subsequently called Santa Francesca Romana. And in this church, after various vicissitudes, it is preserved to this day.

But the surprising story of the *Hodigítria* does not end here.

A tradition that made its way into print at the beginning of the 1800s recounts how Baldwin II, the last Latin emperor of the East, while fleeing from Constantinople in 1261, brought with him the head of the *Hodigítria* and adds that this relic, passed on by inheritance to the Anjou family, prompted the creation, by members of that same Anjou line, of the large Marian icon in the sanctuary of Montevergine near Avellino.[35] Scholars have long since noted that the wood on which the head and halo of the Virgin were painted was

---

[35] Cf. N. M. Laudisio, *Sinossi della diocesi di Policastro*, ed. G. G. Visconti, Thesaurus ecclesiarum Italiae recentioris aevi, vol. 12, no. 3 (Rome, 1976).

of a different kind and that only in the face of the Virgin did traces of an older picture appear—beneath the layer of the medieval picture. All of them were convinced, however, that the tradition was simply a pretty fable. Now, the unexpected conclusion that in the icon of Santa Francesca Romana we can identify the face of the *Hodigítria*—reproduced as a mirror image—offered a new and extremely interesting argument for evaluating the icon of Montevergine. It was necessary to compare the image (turned over, of course) of the head in Rome with that of the head in Montevergine. An eventual coincidence would take on a great significance.

When the two heads were compared, they proved to coincide perfectly; they corresponded practically down to the millimeter. This factual evidence combines with the other indications already noted (diversity of wood, traces of an older picture only under the head of the Madonna) to demonstrate that the "legend" of Baldwin can be considered a striking reality. Other information, which I have gathered and elucidated, confirm that the fugitive king really did carry away with him the head of the *Hodigítria*, that is, as I have explained, the circle containing the "portrait" executed by "Luke". And it is logical to suppose that, in committing that pious theft, he intended to bring with him—along with the head of the *Hodigítria*, patroness of the empire—the hope of his own return, in the not-too-distant future, to Constantinople, to the city that was so dear to the Blessed Virgin. It is quite clear now that the sacred circle containing the head of Mary, painted larger than life, accounts for the creation of an icon of unusual magnitude both in Constantinople and also in Montevergine.

In conclusion, it can be stated that within the icon of Montevergine is preserved, thanks to a series of exceptional developments, the original head of the *Hodigítria*. It is hidden, however, and perhaps will remain so forever, by the restoration of the medieval painter, which inevitably distorted its original features. These features are revealed, nevertheless, thanks to other no less extraordinary developments, in the icon of Santa Francesca Romana.

To Rome, then, belongs the privilege of being able to offer to the eyes of the faithful and of scholars the true likeness of what is (I repeat) to this day the oldest "portrait" of Mary. And this is yet another notable "primacy".

4. THE OLDEST CHRISTIAN STATUE

In speaking of the oldest Christian statue that is known today, I am not thinking of statuettes of smaller dimensions that are part of sacred furnishings or ornamentation, but rather of true statues, in the strict sense, that are on a realistic scale or even, as the case may be, larger than life. Immediately a reflection of a general character comes to mind. In order to find the oldest Christian statue, it would be a mistake to turn to the Eastern world. Evident there, indeed, since the beginning of Christianity, was a decided and long-lasting aversion to introducing statues into the practice of a religion that was so exaltedly spiritual as the one that Christ had founded on earth.

Therefore we need to turn to the West, and here again we immediately notice that Rome holds a "primacy".

For a long time scholars have maintained that the oldest Christian statue was—still at Rome—the marble statue to which was attributed the name of Saint Hippolytus, the renowned doctor of the Church, the statue that today serves as an *ostiaria* [doorkeeper] at the entrance to the Vatican Library. The attribution was so sure as to make some think that the holy doctor had posed for his portrait! With that, those scholars traced the supposedly oldest Christian statue back to the first half of the third century.

But the brilliant idea of those scholars is, today, untenable, because poor "Saint Hippolytus" has at last been "demolished".

I myself am the cause of this noisy "demolition". By successive investigations and intensive research carried out between 1974 and 1989, I believe that I have demonstrated, in fact, that the statue as we see it today is a "pastiche" created in Rome between 1564 and 1565 by that genial and open-minded individual named Pirro Ligorio. Material contributions to the "pastiche" were made by two pieces of female statuary from antiquity and, as models and inspirations, the famous bronze statue of Saint Peter venerated in the Vatican basilica, and also—for the head—an ancient coin (probably counterfeit) that is part of the rich collection of the humanist Fulvio Orsini.[36]

It is necessary, therefore, to abandon the so-called Saint Hippolytus and to turn our attention elsewhere.

The road that we have to travel is not long. Some of my recent research, in fact, has led us to recognize the oldest Christian statue precisely in the famous bronze Saint Peter of the Vatican basilica (figure 9). Everyone knows it. It is located in the central nave near the first pillar on the right in the transept. For centuries visitors to the church have turned their gaze to it, and some even bow before it to kiss the outstretched foot. The statue is found today in the place where Paul V put it around 1620, toward the end of his pontificate

---

[36] M. Guarducci, in *Rendiconti della Pontificia Accademia Romana di Archeologia* 47 (1974–1975): 163–90; idem, in *Ricerche su Ippolito*, Studia Ephemeridis "Augustinianum", 13 (Rome, 1977), pp. 17–30; idem, in *Nuove ricerche su Ippolito*, Studia Ephemeridis "Augustinianum", 30 (Rome, 1989): 61–74.

(1605–1621), but it has behind it, as I will soon explain, a rather long history. Meanwhile let us take a closer look at the famous relic.

The apostle is represented slightly larger than life. Seated on a throne of white marble, the whiteness of which contrasts with the warm tone of the bronze, he wears a tunic and a pallium, raises his right hand in the customary gesture of the orator and the teacher, which can take on, in a Christian context, the significance of a blessing, whereas the left hand, held to his chest, clasps the symbolic keys. On his feet are the sandals that were typical in antiquity of philosophers and schoolmasters.

I have said that the statue has behind it various vicissitudes, and these are, naturally, the equivalent of a long tradition of veneration. As centuries passed, they contributed to its ornamentation. The marble throne is from the 1400s; the base was remade in the 1600s. In the nineteenth century, at the time of Pius IX, a considerable amount of decoration was added, whereas in our [twentieth] century Paul VI has placed in front of the statue two showy bronze lampstands.

But where does the revered Saint Peter come from, and what precisely is its age?

The first explicit mention of it is found in a page written by Maffeo Vegio, who between 1455 and 1457, shortly before his death, composed a treatise concerning the most notable antiquities of the Vatican basilica.[37] According to Vegio, the statue was found at one time in the oratory

[37] Maffeo Vegio, in *Acta Sanctorum*, vol. 7, 2 June (Antwerp, 1717), pp. 61–85 (edited by Corrado Ianninck, in Latin, *Ianningus*); R. Valentini, G. Zucchetti, *Codice topografico della città di Roma*, vol. 4 (Rome, 1953), pp. 377–98. The passage that is of special interest here is in *Acta Sanctorum*, pp. 80f.; Valentini and Zucchetti, *Codice*, pp. 388f.

of San Martino, the most eminent of the monastic com-
plexes that existed near the apse of the original basilica constructed by Constantine, and in that oratory our Saint Peter
had enjoyed fervent veneration on the part of the faithful.
Later on the statue is said to have been transferred to the
basilica, more precisely, to the chapel of Saints Processo
and Martiniano, a chapel that formed part of the ancient
transept. It should be noted in this connection that the two
titular saints were closely associated with Peter. In fact, according to a well-founded tradition, they had been the apostle's jailers when he was imprisoned in the Mamertine jail
and, after being converted and baptized by him, had followed him in the supreme trial of martyrdom. Then, when
the chapel of the holy jailers became involved in the work
being done for the new Renaissance basilica, the bronze
statue found refuge under the splendid organ that Alexander VI, the Borgia pope (1492–1503), had donated to the
basilica itself. The transfer took place between 1534 and
1535, at the beginning of the pontificate of Paul III. Around
the year 1620, toward the end of the pontificate of Paul V,
the statue arrived, as I said, at its present location.

But (and this is for us the most important problem) to
what era does the famous Saint Peter go back? The statue is
certainly older, and not by a little, with respect to the time
of Maffeo Vegio, who speaks of it with the respect due to a
venerable relic. Nevertheless it is natural to want to determine more precisely the date of its origin.

Few problems have aroused more lively disputes among
scholars. Until 1890 the prevailing opinion was that the large
bronze was a work of late antiquity (the fourth through the
sixth century). Then, in 1890 to be exact, a German scholar,
Franz Wickhoff, noisily launched a controversial hypothesis;
namely, that the statue had come from the hands of the fa-

mous Tuscan artist Arnolfo di Cambio, who worked in Rome sometime between 1277 and 1300. This latest idea, based almost exclusively upon reasons of a stylistic sort, was quickly asserted, persuading many partisans both abroad and also in Italy. Here [in Italy] the theory was held by famous art historians such as Adolfo Venturi and Mario Salmi. Angiola Maria Romanini still tenaciously maintains it.

But the Arnolfian hypothesis is definitely untenable. I think that I have demonstrated this in two recent works.[38] It should be sufficient to cite three of the arguments opposed to it: (1) a bronze statuette, clearly a copy of our Saint Peter, was discovered in distant Pakistan and cannot, for obvious reasons, be considered later than the seventh century; (2) a medieval seal attests that in 1283, at the time of Arnolfo, the famous bronze statue was considered "ancient" (*antiqua*); (3) another medieval seal, which is unquestionably a reproduction of the same statue, suggests a line of reasoning from which we can conclude that the famous statue was already in the basilica at the beginning of the thirteenth century, that is, several decades before Arnolfo came into the world. We can deduce instead, with a high degree of probability, that the statue was transferred from the monastery of San Martino to the basilica during the pontificate of Innocent III (1198–1216).

But the most pressing matter here (I repeat) is to establish with greater precision the age of the statue. Here, too, I must cite my recent investigations, from which it is clear that the hypothesis dating it to late antiquity is truly the correct one. Furthermore, my research has led to a conclusion that is entirely new and undeniably suggestive, which I cannot pass over here in silence. Here it is in brief.

---

[38] M. Guarducci, in *Xenia* 16 (1988): 57–72; idem, *San Pietro e Sant'Ippolito, storia di statue famose in Vaticano* (Istituto Poligrafico e Zecca dello Stato, 1991).

The statue originally belonged to the mausoleum of the
Roman emperors of the West, situated in the immediate vicinity of the Constantine basilica, toward the south. There,
the bronze Saint Peter took on an ornamental function and
also a devotional quality. Its size and its exquisite workman-
ship rendered it worthy of such imperial surroundings (which
were supremely ostentatious), whereas the very figure of the
apostle, keeper of the keys of Paradise, assured eternal happiness to the rulers who in that mausoleum, near the tomb
of the apostle himself, awaited the Last Judgment. With that
we may trace the period in which the statue was made back
to the first half of the fifth century, probably even to the
beginning of the century. Indeed, it is probable that the noble edifice was prepared by Honorius, the first emperor of
the West, in the year 404 or a little after; he had been named
emperor in 393 by his father, Theodosius [I], and immediately took up permanent residence at Rome and wore imperial vesture, with his extremely young spouse, Maria, the
daughter of Stilicho, at his side. It is logical, besides, that the
first ruler of the empire of the West should immediately have
wanted to imitate the example of Constantinople, where at
Constantine's command an imperial mausoleum had arisen,
the *Apostoleion*, sanctified by the (alleged) remains of the Eastern apostles. A decision of this sort was all the more logical
on the part of Honorius, inasmuch as he alone had the privilege of being able to construct an imperial mausoleum in
the immediate vicinity of the authentic tomb of Peter, the
Prince of the Apostles. However that may be, the fact remains that the mausoleum of the Vatican received the remains of Maria, the prematurely deceased wife of Honorius,
sometime before 408, and then gradually those of other members of the imperial family, among whom were Honorius
himself, Galla Placidia, and Valentinian III.

After the fall of the Roman Empire in the West (476), and following other developments, the Vatican mausoleum attracted at a certain moment, precisely because of its imperial associations, the most lively interest of the kings of France, who made themselves out to be the legitimate heirs of the defunct Western empire. It was specifically at the request of King Pepin that, in 757, at the beginning of his pontificate, Pope Paul I solemnly transferred from the cemetery of Domitilla to the mausoleum the sarcophagus containing the remains of Saint Petronilla, who was believed to be the daughter, or at least the spiritual daughter, of the apostle Peter, and she very quickly became the patroness of the French. Now, it is extremely likely that this "translation" was prompted by the presence of the large and impressive statue of the apostle in the mausoleum. The supposed father Peter seems, in short, to have been the summons for the venerated relics of Petronilla, his supposed daughter. There is even a legend that Peter, having survived his daughter, carved with his own hand the sepulchral epigraph or inscription on the sarcophagus containing her remains. After about a century the famous statue seems to have been transferred to the adjoining monastery of San Martino, perhaps in 846, with the purpose of guarding it from the violence of the Saracens, who indeed in that year sacked the Vatican basilica. And it cannot be a simple coincidence that France was present in the monastery of San Martino as well. Martin, in fact, the holy bishop of Tours, was the patron of the French, just as Petronilla was their patroness.

The great bronze statue of Saint Peter seems to have been cast in Rome, perhaps executed by, or with the collaboration of, those Antiochene artisans who were universally recognized as being highly skilled in the art of bronze. Let it be noted also, in this connection, that the characteristic "spiral" curls [*ricci "a lumachelle"*], quite visible in the hair and on the beard of our Saint Peter, are clearly comparable to those in certain Antiochene and Palmyran sculptures, and especially in a marble head preserved today in Paris in the Louvre Museum, a work that scholars not arbitrarily attribute to Antioch and date to the first half of the fifth century.[39] Then too, it is not strange at all that a refined work of art such as the statue of Saint Peter could be executed in Rome toward the beginning of the fifth century. Under the auspices of the Roman emperors of the West, art would still be flourishing in the Roman workshops. One proof of this, among others, is a superb bust of the empress Licinia Eudoxia that, according to my recent research, was executed in Rome in 450 and that reveals a technical expertise that is difficult to attain.[40]

At any rate, our primary interest here is the proof that the great bronze Saint Peter belongs to the beginning of the fifth century. This dating means, in turn, that we are dealing with the oldest Christian statue among those that are known today: another "primacy" of which the Church of Rome can boast.

5. THE OLDEST CHRISTIAN RELIC THAT IS CERTAINLY AUTHENTIC: THE BONES OF PETER IN THE VATICAN BASILICA

A fifth and extraordinary "primacy" that the Catholic Church of Rome has with respect to the other Christian Churches is

[39] F. Coche de la Ferté, *L'Antiquité chrétienne au Musée du Louvre* (Paris, 1958), p. 11, n. 3.

[40] My essay [was as of 1991] in the process of being published in the *Bulletino della Commissione Archeologica Comunale di Roma*.

that of possessing the sole demonstrably authentic relic of one of the twelve apostles: that of Peter in the Vatican basilica.

When we speak of a relic, it can refer to the remains of a saint's body or to objects that belonged to holy persons or that took part in some memorable and holy action. Here we are speaking, of course, about the remains of a body, and (we must acknowledge it at the outset) it is impressive that the sole relic in the world that can be identified with certainty as having belonged to a holy man who had known Christ and had been present at his miracles is precisely that of Peter.

Over the centuries of history, not a few relics were attributed to the venerable persons of the apostles and as such were exposed to the devotion of the faithful in various parts of the Christian world. In this sense, relics of Andrew, of James, and also of Peter are known. Very often it is a matter of little pieces of cloth (*brandea*) that had been touched to their respective tombs, or were supposed to have been, according to a medieval custom of which Pope Gregory the Great (590–604), as is well known, was an authoritative defender—in Rome. Besides these "relics" consisting of pieces of cloth, however, there was no lack of other "relics" of the apostles consisting of skeletal fragments. I am thinking, in particular, of the "relics" of Andrew. But (I repeat) only of Peter are true relics (without the quotation marks) still in existence, and these are found in Rome in the Vatican basilica.

The very learned Belgian scholar of hagiography Father Hippolyte Delehaye, whose works are still authoritative, published in 1934 a classic study concerning the relics of the saints. In these pages from his pen he correctly enunciates and illustrates with appropriate examples a fundamental rule: namely, that in order to establish the authenticity of a relic one needs above all to know with precision where it came from and that this provenance cannot be, in the final analysis, anything but the tomb of the venerated personage.[41]

Well, now, we do not know exactly the tomb of any of the apostles, with the exception of Peter. This is the unique exception, which cries out for attention. It follows from a concatenation of dates of various sorts, a concatenation (we must admit) that is too unusual to be considered the product of chance.

The great or even—I should say—vital importance of the subject induces me to repeat here in summary form information that I have already presented many times and explained extensively.

Peter came to Rome in order to bring to the capital of that empire, which identified itself with the known world at that time, the good news entrusted to him by Christ. At Rome he died a martyr in the persecution of Nero (A.D. 64). His martyrdom took place in the Circus of Nero on the Vatican Hill, where Peter was crucified, following also in the manner of his execution the example of his Master. Within the Vatican Hill itself, near the place of his martyrdom, the apostle was buried. In connection with the tomb of Peter in Rome, it is interesting to note that its presence *in Urbe* (in the city) is implicitly confirmed by the circumstance that no other city besides Rome ever boasted of possessing it.

Over the tomb of Peter, which was hollowed out of the ground and was certainly known and revered from the beginning, there arose in the following century, and more precisely in the second half of it, a small but dignified sepulchral monument. Still later, in the third decade of the fourth cen-

---

[41] H. Delehaye, *Cinq leçons sur la méthode hagiographique*, Susidia hagiographica, vol. 21 (Brussels, 1934), pp. 75–116. The passage that is of interest here is at p. 76.

tury, the emperor Constantine commanded the first basilica in honor of Peter to be constructed over his tomb. A persistent tradition, furthermore, noted that the tomb of the apostle was located beneath the altar of the confession, that is, beneath the altar that even today is the papal altar of the Vatican basilica.

All of this was established with precision even before the excavations contributed the findings of archaeology to the solution of the great problem. These excavations, which were carried out at the request of Pius XII between 1940 and 1949, essentially confirmed the tradition, even though they developed in a manner that was quite unusual. Beneath the altar of the confession was found the site of the ancient earthen tomb, surmounted by a small funeral monument from the second century. It was ascertained, furthermore, that upon this monument others had come to be added over the course of the centuries, thus splendidly demonstrating the continuity of the cult of Peter on that precise spot of the Vatican Hill. Indeed, superimposed upon the monument of the second century were: the monument that Constantine ordered to be constructed in honor of the apostle even before he set about building the basilica; the altar of Gregory the Great (590–604); the altar of Callistus II (consecrated in 1123); the altar of Clement VIII (consecrated in 1594). The burial of Peter had taken place near the Circus, beyond the road that ran alongside it in ancient times, dividing it from the slope of the Vatican Hill. The excavations ascertained likewise that the earthen tomb of Peter came to be included within a vast and rich necropolis (originally pagan), which was formed in the second and third centuries along the way that ran alongside the Circus. In ancient Rome it was a normal practice for cemeteries to develop along the roads that led out from the city walls. In this way it was possible to determine that, in order to erect the basilica in honor of Peter in the place indicated by his tomb, it was necessary to fill up with earth a part of the necropolis that was still in use and furthermore to cut away a piece of the Vatican Hill: these were very serious decisions that only the will of an emperor was in a position to make; they clearly prove the enormous importance of that compelling spot, the tomb of the apostle.

But here a strange thing happened, at least apparently: a circumstance that was quite unthinkable and unforeseeable. That supremely important place, which everything concurred in identifying as the ancient tomb of Peter, was empty: the expected relics of the martyr seemed to have vanished into thin air. Later it fell to me, without any warning whatsoever, to resolve the astonishing enigma. I did indeed track down the remaining bones of Peter and finally identified them as such, while taking the utmost care to employ the most rigorous scientific method. I will not attempt here to recount at length the almost adventurous developments that led me to the unexpected result; I will say only that I succeeded at last in understanding how things had happened.

I have said already that, immediately before building the basilica in honor of Peter, the emperor Constantine made arrangements so that upon the site of the ancient tomb, where there was already a funereal monument from the second century, a new and more magnificent monument might arise. This, practically speaking, was superimposed upon the preceding one, or better, included it within the new design and enriched it with a style of ornamentation that was more in keeping with the dignity of the Prince of the Apostles. On that occasion the intention was (logically enough) to secure a new and definitive arrangement of the famous relics, which were still lying in the bare earth. The bones that still remained, or at least were still visible, were gathered from the earth, wrapped in a precious cloth of purple interwoven with gold, and placed in a niche that had been suitably prepared in the interior of the monument dedicated to the apostle. To make this niche they used a wall that already existed on-site, which belonged to a small construction annexed—in the third century—to the old second-century monument. This is the wall conventionally referred to as "wall g". It had been excavated enough to form the niche from it, which was then lined with marble slabs. Above the opening to the tomb remained then a stretch of the wall, and this was covered by an impressive network, a veritable thicket, of Christian grafitti; the overcrowding itself demonstrated the immense veneration that the faithful gave to this sacred place between the end of the third century and the construction by Constantine (figure 10).

The decision to take the venerable bones out of the ground and to enclose them within the monument probably had the purpose of removing those remains from the dreadful humidity of a place that was notoriously subject to the action of rainwater and of subterranean streams. As for the cloth that was used to wrap up the bones, note that the purple and the gold were associated with the majesty of sovereigns and were in keeping therefore with the imperial porphyry with which the exterior of the monument was decorated.

Eusebius, bishop of Caesarea, who lived at the time of Constantine and was also in personal contact with him, in his work *Theophania* (composed around 333, that is, before the death of the ruler), described the monument erected by the latter in honor of Peter as "a splendid sepulcher".[42] The description is exact in every way, because this monument truly contained the mortal remains of the apostle.

---

[42] Eusebius, *Theophania* 4, 7, ed. H. Gressmann (Leipzig, 1964), p. 175.

The marble niche of the Constantinian monument was therefore the second tomb of Peter, and it remained intact and inviolate until it was opened, which took place, it seems, in 1941. Strangely, having escaped the attention of the archaeologists (as I said, the procedures followed during the excavations were not at all normal) and after being removed from the niche without their knowledge, the bones of Peter remained unknown for more than ten years inside a plain wooden box in a storeroom of the Vatican Grotto. Thanks to a series of fortunate circumstances, I discovered them in 1953, but did not recognize them immediately. Only in 1963, thanks to another series of fortunate developments, I identified them and immediately determined to devote a scholarly paper to them. The final publication appeared in 1965.[43]

The prerequisite condition established by Fr. Delehaye in his day for declaring the authenticity of a relic, namely, the certainty that it came from the respective tomb, is entirely fulfilled in the case of the relics of Peter. Added to this is the extraordinary convergence of the results of tests to which the bones and the materials of various sorts that accompanied it were subjected, at my instigation, by practitioners of the respective experimental sciences. The mortal remains of Peter, therefore, had to be considered authentic for all intents and purposes.

Peter (I repeat) is the only apostle whose authentic relics have come down to us, and these relics are found precisely in Rome, in the Vatican basilica, in what is the center and heart of the Catholic Church.

We are dealing, then, with exceptionally substantial relics: all told, about one half of the skeleton. Note, too, that all

---

[43] M. Guarducci, *Le reliquie di Pietro sotto la Confessione della Basilica Vaticana* (Vatican City, 1965).

parts of the body are represented, with the exception of the feet. The complete lack of any sort of bony fragment belonging to the feet can perhaps acquire some significance when one thinks of the sort of martyrdom (crucifixion) that Peter had to undergo. If this is correct, it would constitute another proof, if indeed we still needed one, of the authenticity of the famous relic.

On this point, someone might observe that in Rome there was already known *ab antiqua* [from antiquity], outside the Vatican, a famous relic of Peter. I mean the "skull of Saint Peter", which for centuries has been venerated beside the "skull of Saint Paul" in the Lateran basilica. But—let it be said immediately—we are dealing here with "relics" (in quotation marks) belonging to the great crowds of medieval objects exposed to the devotion of the faithful; objects that are venerable for the salutary thoughts and the virtuous actions to which they have so often given rise, but—let us say it outright—definitely spurious.

The problem with the "skull of Saint Peter" presented itself, naturally and quite urgently, in the course of the investigations carried out, as I said, upon the bones coming from the niche of the Constantine monument. The problem of the "Lateran skull" appeared all the more necessary and urgent, inasmuch as the bones found in the niche included numerous fragments from the skull as well. Since Peter, obviously, could not have had two skulls, a comparison was inevitable between the cranial bones discovered in the niche and the "skull" contained in the Lateran reliquary. It was a propitious occasion for examining also the "skull of Saint Paul". The two reliquaries were transported to the Vatican, and here investigations were carried out with the customary and uncompromising scientific rigor. The conclusion was definitely negative for the "Lateran skulls". Besides, it cannot be denied that these relics are recorded in history for the first time in the eleventh century and that in that era the search for and hence the commerce in relics (or objects believed to be such) was in full flower, both in the East and in the West. I have had more than one occasion to speak about this experience with respect to the "skulls" of the two apostles.

But now it is time to turn to the authentic relics of Peter, which are (it is helpful to repeat) only those found in the Vatican basilica. This is a distinction that prompts reflection and leads us at last, almost necessarily, to acknowledge an—I would say—arcane title to spiritual primacy for the Church of Rome.

No less important and worth meditating upon is the circumstance that this unique distinction pertains precisely to Peter.

Who, indeed, is Peter? He is the apostle who, in and of himself, evokes in our mind the concept of primacy.

In the official list of the twelve apostles that has been handed down to us by the evangelist Matthew, "Simon, who is called Peter" bears the title of the "first" ($\pi\varrho\tilde{\omega}\tau o\varsigma$),[44] and not without reason. Indeed, Christ himself, at the beginning of his public life, had conferred that priority upon Peter, and later, on various occasions, explicitly or implicitly, he willed to confirm his prerogative.

The first encounter of Jesus with Peter had taken place on the sea of Tiberias. Simon, who is called Peter, the fisherman, together with his brother Andrew were casting a net into the water when Jesus commanded them to abandon their nets and boat and to follow him, promising that he would make them fishers of men.[45] But very soon the primacy was

[44] Mt 10:2.
[45] Mt 4:18–19; Mk 1:16–17.

definitively assigned to Peter, and this occurred by the explicit will of Christ himself.

The most famous and eloquent recognition that Christ willed to give to Peter is found in the dialogue that developed between the Master and the apostle at Caesarea Philippi. The well-known episode is related only by the Gospel of Matthew.[46] Peter, by divine inspiration, acknowledges that Jesus is the Christ, Son of the living God, and then Jesus answers him with the celebrated words: "You are Peter, and on this rock I will build my church, and the powers of death shall not prevail against it. I will give you the keys of the kingdom of heaven, and whatever you bind on earth shall be bound in heaven, and whatever you loose on earth shall be loosed in heaven." This signifies, with the utmost clarity, that Peter will have to represent Christ on earth and to possess on earth his own divine authority.

So great was the significance of this passage that it has inevitably aroused doubts and dissension on the part of those who tend to diminish the importance of Peter in the history of Christianity. Some have attempted to maintain absolutely that the entire passage was interpolated later on, as an afterthought, into the text of the Gospel. It is indisputable, however, that the words, "Tu es Petrus", together with what follows, prove that Christ intended Peter to have the primacy over the other apostles.[47]

---

[46] Mt 16:17–19.

[47] On this passage, cf., among others, O. Cullmann (*Petrus, Apostel-Jünger-Märtyrer*, 2d ed. [Zürich-Stuttgart, 1960], pp. 183–271), who thinks that Christ had intended to confer the authority upon Peter alone, and not to his successors, and for a limited period of his life (see the conclusions of the over-long discussion at p. 271). An analogous thought had been expressed by Tertullian in his Montanist period (see above, p. 41).

In other passages of the Gospels, Jesus shows that he attributes a particular importance to Peter. According to the Gospel of Luke, he permits Peter alone to walk upon the water, so as to give to him and to the others proof that he, Jesus, is truly the Son of God.[48] Likewise, without naming Peter, he surely alludes to him when—in the Gospel of Luke—he speaks of the wise steward, whom the master places in charge of his household until the time of his own return.[49] He addresses Peter directly, though, when, again in the Gospel of Luke, he states that he has prayed that Peter might remain firm in the faith required to sustain and strengthen his brothers.[50] On the other hand, in the Gospel of John, during his appearance to the disciples by the sea of Tiberias, Jesus commends the flock to Peter alone with the impassioned plea to feed his lambs.[51]

Then, in the Gospel of Matthew, there is a passage indicating that Christ considered Peter not only the first among the others, but also the apostle most closely associated to himself, as though raised to his own level. This is the well-known episode in which Jesus orders Peter to pay the temple tribute for both of them with the stater (a coin worth two drachmas) that he would find in the mouth of the fish he would capture on a fishhook.[52] But I will have the occasion to return to this passage a little farther on.[53]

The preeminence of Peter, decisively proclaimed by Christ, is recognized (and it could not have been otherwise) by the

[48] Mt 14:24–31.
[49] Lk 12:35–48.
[50] Lk 22:31.
[51] Jn 21:15–17.
[52] Mt 17:24–27.
[53] See below, p. 120.

other disciples as well. Thus, in the Gospel of John we read that Mary Magdalen, having found the tomb open, ran immediately to Peter and to the other disciple whom Jesus loved, that is, to John himself, to tell them about the tremendous event.[54] We read also that John, who arrived first at the tomb, did not enter it immediately but waited for the arrival of Peter, who was running after him. And Peter was indeed the one who first entered the tomb and first saw the unexpected scene with the linen wrappings lying about and the *sudarium* [the cloth that had been on his head] folded up to one side, while there was no trace of the body of Jesus.[55]

Paul, too, the apostle who had not known Christ but who had been chosen by Christ himself to spread the good news, openly confirmed the preeminence of Peter. After being converted miraculously on the road to Damascus by the dazzling apparition of the Redeemer, he traveled to Jerusalem in order to consult with Peter and remained with him for fifteen days, obviously recognizing in Peter the head of the Christian community.[56] He himself, then, in his first letter to the Corinthians, probably written in the year 57, quite a few years before the Gospel of John was composed, spoke of the Resurrection and of its capital importance for Christians, and he did not hesitate to declare that the Risen One appeared first to Peter, then to the other apostles, then to more than five hundred other brothers, and finally to Paul himself.[57] Here too, then, Peter occupies, as always, the first place.

[54] Jn 20:2.
[55] Jn 20:6–7.
[56] Gal 1:18.
[57] 1 Cor 15:5–8.

In a word, Peter undeniably possesses a primacy, by Christ's own designation and by the unanimous acknowledgment of his brethren. Well, now, it is precisely this Peter whose mortal remains, by way of exception, have come down to us, and these remains have been authenticated by science.

The tradition concerning the presence of Peter's tomb in Rome in the Vatican basilica has been for centuries the great stumbling block for the adversaries of the Church of Rome and of her primacy. Now, not only the presence of the tomb but also the presence of the apostle's relics has become, for every person with right judgment, factual data.

This is a further "primacy" of incalculable importance that the Church of Rome possesses and in which it is difficult not to recognize the intervention—as I would put it—of a mysterious will.

6. THE MONOGRAMS OF THE UNION
OF CHRIST AND PETER

I have already said that in the New Testament Peter is considered by Christ himself the first of the apostles and that the other apostles also recognized him as such. I have furthermore recalled that one passage from the Gospel of Matthew attests to the will of Christ to associate Peter to himself, to place him almost at his own level.[58] We mean the well-known passage in which Christ orders Peter to pay the temple tribute for both of them, using the stater that he would find in the fish's mouth.[59]

---

[58] See above, p. 118, and below, pp. 124–25.
[59] See above, p. 118.

One may wonder now whether the concept of a special and intimate bond between the Master and the first of the apostles, of a spiritual *societas* between the two, was at least taken up again and confirmed outside of the Gospel text.

Here, too, Rome immediately stands out and, as far as I know, only Rome.

The concept that I have mentioned is manifested many times, and with the utmost clarity, on the surface of wall *g*, that precious wall covered with graffiti, which, as I explained, was included in the Constantinian monument in honor of Peter beneath the altar of the confession and in which was carved the niche destined to contain the remaining bones of the apostle.[60]

In the dense network of graffiti engraved on that wall, above the niche, the name of Peter appears many times (expressed in abbreviated form: P or PE or PET), which is often associated with the monogram of Christ ☧ and with the name of Mary (M or MA or even—in its entirety—MARIA), in a common acclamation of victory (N or NA or even NIKA and NICA [Greek for "he conquers"]).

In elucidating these graffiti in the second volume of the work entitled *I graffiti sotto la Confessione di San Pietro in Vaticano* [The graffiti beneath the altar of the confession in Saint Peter's at the Vatican], which was published in 1958, I always spoke of the "association" between Peter and Christ.[61] There are, however, among others, three graffiti in which the association seems to be transformed into an even closer bond. It is not impertinent, I think, to mention again here the three texts and to turn now to consider them with due attention.

---

[60] See above, pp. 112–13.

[61] M. Guarducci, *I graffiti sotto la Confessione di San Pietro in Vaticano* (Vatican City, 1958), 3 vol.

1. On the wall with the inscriptions, to the upper left, is engraved, in large letters, the name of the deceased *Leonia* preceded by the monogram of Christ:[62]

☧ LEONIA

True to the custom, demonstrated quite plainly by the graffiti on wall *g*, of enriching spiritually these texts with a system of mystical cryptography, the author of the *Leonia* graffito, too, wanted to adorn the name that he wrote with precious, significant, and consoling additions.

First of all, above the ✗ he inscribed the famous motto referring to the vision of Constantine: *hoc vinc[e]* ("conquer with this", that is, with the name of Christ).[63] Thus we are able to determine the date of the graffito: after October 28, 312, the day of Constantine's victory by the Milvian Bridge, and before the inclusion of wall *g* into the Constantine monument, that is, between around 321 and 326.

Another addition to our graffito, an addition that takes on particular interest here, consists of an E clearly placed at the head of the *rho* of the monogram ✗:[64]

This addition suffices to express the concept of the indissoluble union between Christ and Peter. In bestowing upon the Greek letter *rho* a secondary value, that of the Latin letter

---

[62] Ibid., 2:6–75, n. 2.
[63] Ibid., 2:14 (cf. p. 33).
[64] Ibid., 2:7–10.

p, the author of the graffito wanted to say that Christ (☧) and Peter (PE) are closely united to each other.

Furthermore, the L of *Leonia* that follows the ☧ was transfigured into the monogram of Peter, which represented at the same time his symbolic key; and before the monograms of Christ and Peter was inscribed the preposition *in*

which resulted in the wish (referring to the deceased) that she might participate in the life of Christ and of Peter; included in this wish is also the thought of the key to the kingdom of heaven that Peter keeps.[65]

Then, ingeniously written between the monograms of Christ and Peter were the words DVX LVX PAX LEX (leader, light, peace, law), portentous monosyllabic words that refer to Christ, but that indirectly pertain to Peter as well.[66]

I will forego mentioning here the other "embroideries" that were obtained employing the remaining letters of the name *Leonia*.

2. To the right of the graffito *Leonia*, there is a mystical concatenation of salutary letters belonging to the names of four deceased persons; one man and three women (Verus, Bonifatia, Venerosa, Vea). At the top of this chain we can read an acclamation of victory (NICA) addressed to Christ (☧), Peter (PE), and Mary (MARIA).[67]

---

[65] Ibid., 2:41f.
[66] Ibid., 2:49f. (cf. pp. 48–65).
[67] Ibid., 2:131, n. 15 (cf. pp. 116–51).

Here, too, as in the *Leonia* graffito, the *rho* of the monogram of Christ (P) functions also as the *p* of the Petrine monogram, specifying, together with the E added at its right, the name of the apostle (PE). Here once again appears the concept of the intimate, indissoluble union of Peter with Christ.

3. At the far end of the inscribed wall, at the upper right, appears in isolation the monogram of Christ, expressed this time with the letters CHRS = *Chr*[*istu*]*s*.

Here, too, the fondness for alphabetical symbolism is at work. This is demonstrated by the transformation of the letter H into A, the symbol of life, and the insertion of a monogram of Peter (PE in abbreviated form).[68] The insertion of the letter *p* signifies, evidently, the usual intention of associating the name of Peter closely with that of Christ and of representing thereby the extremely close union of the two celestial figures.

The repeated association of Peter to Christ is perfectly in keeping with the place in which the inscribed wall is found, near the most venerable tomb of the apostle, in the heart of the Vatican basilica. It will be useful to recall, at this point, a thought of Saint Augustine, which he expressed at the beginning of the fifth century.[69] Speaking precisely of the *memoria* of Peter in Rome, that is, of the Constantine monument in the Vatican basilica, in which the apostle's tomb was known to exist, Augustine poses this question to himself and to his

---

[68] Ibid., 2:114f., n. 14 (cf. pp. 111–16).
[69] Augustine, *Enarrationes in Psalmos* 44, 23.

readers: "Who is honored in Peter, if not he who died for us?" To honor Peter, then, means to honor Christ. Saint Augustine could not have acknowledged more effectively the close, indissoluble union between the Master and the first of his disciples, that union that the ancient graffiti, of which he was ignorant, had intended to express right in that holy place.

Several years before I deciphered the graffiti of wall *g*, antiquarians at Rome knew of a small slab of marble that had been discovered in an unknown cemetery site and was then preserved in the Lateran Museum of Sacred Art.[70] Inscribed upon this marble is the monogram ⳩, with an E balanced upon the head of the *rho*, the very same motif that appears in the *Leonia* graffito[71] (figure 11).

Scholars who in their day examined this slab of marble sought to interpret the singular inscription upon it, but they did not succeed in finding a plausible explanation of it. Today, thanks to the *Leonia* graffito, which at that time was not known, the explanation is clear. We are dealing with the monogram that closely associates the names of Christ and Peter, which is inserted here within the preposition *in*. From it we can derive, in short, good wishes for life in Christ and in Peter, a wish that we must consider as being directed to the unknown deceased person lying in the tomb to which the marble belonged.

A wish not unlike that one is found, though expressed in another way, upon a small slab of marble discovered—once

---

[70] A. Silvagni, *Inscriptiones Christianae Urbis Romae*, new series, vol. 1 (Rome, 1922), no. 1900; Guarducci, *I graffiti*, 1:143–50, fig. 49.

[71] To the right of the monogram, on a smaller scale, it seems possible to distinguish an overturned vase (of the *refrigerium* [cooling waters]?) with the monogram ⳩.

more in Rome—in the cemetery of Praetextatus and missing today, as it seems.[72] On the marble appears, or I should say, appeared a key inserted into the stock of an anchor. Since the key is a symbol of Peter and sometimes, as we have seen, is intended also to express his name in abbreviated form (PE), and since, on the other hand, the anchor is the symbolic image of the salvific Cross of Christ, here again we find ourselves confronted with the graphic expression of the indissoluble union between Christ and Peter.

The graffiti of wall *g* and the two sepulchral monuments that I have described belong to Rome. Nowhere else, as far as I know, do epigraphs exist that clearly illustrate, as these do, the concept of the intimate association between Christ and Peter, which follows—in the Gospel of Matthew—from the episode of the single stater destined to pay the tribute of the Master together with that of the apostle.

The presence of such documents exclusively in Rome can be traced back in the final analysis (it is reasonable to admit) to the tomb of Peter, that is, to what has been for centuries the clearest and most eloquent "primacy" of the Church of Rome.

[72] Guarducci, *I graffiti*, 1:464f., fig. 242.

4

ROME, PREDESTINED CITY

To the Christians of antiquity, Rome appeared to be connected to Christianity by providential signs. Already in the first century, the Acts of the Apostles tell how Christ himself appeared in a dream to Paul to announce to him that, just as he had given testimony to him in Jerusalem, so he would have to testify in Rome as well.[1] And again the same Acts, when they speak of the furious storm that hit Paul during his voyage from Crete to Italy, have an angel of God intervene to assure the apostle that the boat and its passengers would escape the danger unharmed, because it was necessary for Paul "to stand before Caesar", that is, to arrive in Rome.[2] And again much later a learned Father of the Church who lived in Mesopotamia between 451 and 521, Jacob of Sarug, referring in one of his sermons to the apostles, who after the Resurrection left to chance the decision as to the country in which each of them would have to preach the good news, considers it a "divinum ... opus" [divine act] that Rome was assigned to Peter by lot. It was indeed, in his judgment, the will of God that the "firstborn of the brethren", that is, the Prince of the Apostles, should bring the message about Christ to the "mother of all cities",

---

[1] Acts 23:11.
[2] Acts 27:23f.

that is, to Rome.[3] And other citations could be added to this one.

It would seem, then, that there was a mysterious bond between Christianity and Rome. That this is not the product of the imagination is proved, I think, by a more attentive examination of the very development of Rome from its origins to its triumphant apogee. Anyone, indeed, who pauses to meditate a little upon these developments cannot overlook, here and there, certain indications of a mysterious design that had, I should say, prearranged them for the appearance of Christianity in the world.

The essential element in this design is the great Roman Empire, which came to embrace—on the three continents washed by the Mediterranean (Europe, Asia, and Africa)—the entire civilized world that was then known, an empire that had its center precisely in Rome. The idea that this universal empire had been the basis necessary for the spread of Christianity did not escape Christian thinkers. We have already seen that in the second half of the second century Melito, bishop of Sardis, while writing his *Apologia* for the emperor Marcus Aurelius, did not fail to mention the bonds that existed between the empire and the religion of Christ, and he even paused to consider especially the advantages that Christian "philosophy", the "foster-sister" of the empire, had procured for the latter.[4] A full recognition of the providential relation between the empire and Christianity was then given later on, at the beginning of the fifth century, by Paulus Orosius, the renowned writer originally from Tarragona on the Iberian Peninsula, who was a close friend of Saint Augustine. In his great universal history, which goes from

---

[3] Jacob of Sarug, *Sermones* 99.
[4] See above, pp. 22–23.

the beginning of the world to A.D. 417 and which is specifically dedicated to Augustine, Paulus Orosius indeed advances the thesis that the universal empire of Rome had been willed by divine Providence: a thesis that much later played a great part in Dante Alighieri's concept of the universal monarchy.[5]

But how did this providential Roman Empire come into being? To understand this better, it will be useful to go back to an even more remote past.

Before the empire of Rome, the ancient world knew other empires, which one after the other arose, reached their culmination, and declined. A universal empire had been attempted in the fifteenth century B.C. in Egypt by the pharaoh Thutmose III; then followed the empires of Assyria, Babylon, and Persia. The last-mentioned one, in its attempt to expand to the West, had encountered a strong obstacle in Greece, a country that was politically divided, but united in the common cause of making intellectual conquests and by a common love of liberty. Having reached agreement in the face of danger, the Greeks, led by Athens and Sparta, won a tremendous victory over the Persian invaders in 480 B.C., near the little island of Salamina.

But the decisive victory of Greece over Persia took place in the following century through the efforts of the Macedonians and contributed to the establishment of a new empire, that of Alexander the Great; an empire that then had enormous importance also for the history of the future Roman Empire and, consequently, for the spread of Christianity.

---

[5] Orosius develops his ideas on the providential task of Rome in the seven books of his *Historiae contra paganos*. As for Dante, cf. A. Martina, in *Enciclopedia Dantesca*, vol. 4 (Rome, 1973), pp. 204–8.

Apparent here, to anyone who reflects even briefly, is a singular concatenation of events, some of which would have been difficult to foresee. In the second half of the fourth century [B.C.], Philip II, king of Macedonia, at any rate, could scarcely have imagined that his son Alexander would definitively defeat the Persians and found upon the ruins of their empire a new empire, greater yet by far. Against the Persians, it is true, Philip harbored feelings of revenge that prompted him to attack them, but his plans did not make much headway. Besides, not one of his contemporaries felt the impulse to make a grandiose expedition into Asia; even the famous Athenian rhetor Isocrates, who attended the king as his counselor, proposed as the utmost limit of an eventual expansion of Hellenism toward the East a line that would connect the city of Sinope on the Black Sea and Cilicia on the southern coast of Asia Minor.[6]

Quite different, on the other hand, in the second half of the fourth century [B.C.], were the thoughts of Alexander, who in 336 succeeded his father, Philip, who had tragically vanished from the scene. Endowed with strong leadership qualities, inspired by the thrilling stories of the Homeric heroes, eager for glory, Alexander was capable of conceiving and carrying out great enterprises. Within two short years Macedonia had gained—with the victory at Chaeronea (338)—predominance over Greece. Now, in the mind of the youthful king (he was scarcely twenty years old), the idea of a campaign against the Persians beckoned with ever greater insistence.

And behold, he suddenly had himself named, by the Greeks gathered in Corinth, the captain in a holy war against the

---

[6] Isocrates, *Philippus* 120.

Persians (who were guilty of having violated, in their time, the Hellenic sanctuaries), and he immediately went into action. After crossing the Hellespont in the year 334 [B.C.] and overcoming the first resistance of the Persians on the river Granicus, he traversed Asia Minor in a lightning-quick advance, conquered the Persian king Darius III at Issus in Cilicia, went over into Egypt, where he founded a city to which he gave his own name (Alexandria), and visited the oasis consecrated to Zeus Ammon, where he had himself solemnly proclaimed the son of god. Having satisfied the supreme ambition of mounting from the human sphere to that of the gods, the dynamic Alexander returned to Asia, crossed the river Tigris, and at Gaugamela in Assyria he won a tumultuous and decisive victory over the king of Persia. A great empire was now his, and from this stronghold he set his eager sights even farther, toward legendary India, and in one expedition he actually succeeded in reaching its western borders.

Alexander did not survive by very long his almost superhuman enterprise. In 323, in Babylon, he vanished, a little more than thirty years old, from the world scene, in which his brief life had played so great a part. That life had in fact been a prodigy. From it had proceeded, in the final analysis, tremendous developments destined to be of enormous importance in the history of all mankind.

At the untimely death of Alexander, the empire that he had miraculously established was commended into the hands of three of his generals (Antigonus, Seleucus, Ptolemy), who, after quarreling with one another, gradually provoked its dissolution. But meanwhile Greek civilization had extended far and wide in Asia and Egypt, coming into contact with other civilizations and with very ancient religions, from which it in turn had absorbed elements of culture and of wisdom.

Note that the empire of Alexander also included Palestine, the future land of Jesus, which had long since been rooted in the worship of the one supreme God of the universe, a creed that would be the foundation for the religion of Christ.

Once Alexander was dead, his empire, divided among his successors, was shattered. At the right moment, Rome would come, to reestablish its unity—indeed, to enlarge it.

Here, too, we find ourselves confronted with a concatenation of developments that leads us to ponder. How could a tiny village of shepherds become little by little the center of a universal empire, even greater and more powerful than the great and powerful empire of Alexander the Great? It will be useful to trace here, in summary form, the stages of this prodigious development, which extends through more than seven centuries of history, between the day of Rome's founding (according to tradition, 754 B.C.) and the birth of the empire (27 B.C.).

Situated in a hilly area, not far from the sea, the village inhabited by shepherds was transformed gradually into a tiny city ruled by a monarchy, which later became a free republic. We are, with the latter change, in the year 510 B.C.

After victoriously overcoming internal travails and quarrels with neighboring peoples, Rome found itself, at the end of the fifth century B.C., the uncontested mistress of Latium. Recall, in this connection, the poetic tradition according to which the divine Dioscuri, mounted upon their horses, had miraculously appeared during the battle near Lake Regillus to encourage the Romans who were arrayed against the army of the Latin cities, deciding the outcome of the battle, of course, in favor of Rome.

Having become the proprietress of Latium, Rome expanded toward southern Etruria, opposed in vain by the powerful Etruscan city of Veii, which, after a long siege, surrendered in 396 [B.C.]. Lo and behold, after scarcely a decade (386), the arrival of a grave peril. This one was the invasion of the Gauls, the violent barbarians who, having conquered Rome, put it to the sword and set it on fire and did not retreat until they had obtained the payment of a fat ransom. But the Romans did not lose heart: Rome arose again from the ruins and continued its unstoppable ascent.

It was now a question of extending Roman dominion to the rest of the peninsula. A very important stage in this undertaking was the victory won near Sentinum (in what is today the Marches), a victory with which the Romans dealt a mortal blow to the Sanniti and to their Italian allies (295 B.C.). Another decisive stage was the victory won in 275 in Lucania (others place it, less accurately, at Benevento) over Pyrrhus, king of Epirus, who from Greece had intervened in the Italian peninsula and was seriously impeding the expansion of Rome in southern Italy.

At this point Rome, by now ruler of Italy, was in a position to turn all of its forces against a formidable rival: Carthage. This ancient Punic city in northern Africa, founded by the Phoenicians from Tyre, was bound to Rome by two treaties of alliance (the first had been concluded in 509, when the Republic of Rome had scarcely been founded), but now Carthage, having become a great naval power in the western Mediterranean, cast a shadow on the new power of Rome. Thus began the famous Punic Wars.

The First Punic War, which started in 264 [B.C.] and ended in 241 [B.C.], gave the Romans possession of Sicily, an island on which the Carthaginians had exercised their authority overbearingly. Sicily was followed, a little later, by Sardinia and Corsica.

The Second Punic War put Rome to an extremely difficult test. The bold Carthaginian general Hannibal, having crossed the Alps with his army in a daring march that included even the dreaded elephants, traversed the peninsula menacingly, inflicting serious defeats on the Romans (218–216 B.C.). Mortal danger loomed over Rome. But the Romans, with their indomitable will, succeeded in waging war in Africa, so that Hannibal was called back to his native country, and at Zama, to the west of Carthage, they won in 202 [B.C.] that tumultuous victory which forced the Carthaginians to accept harsh terms of peace.

The Third Punic War, which was started in 150 [B.C.], ended in 146 [B.C.] with the complete destruction of Carthage.

Henceforth Rome was mistress of a large part of northern Africa. This was of great importance also for the future spread of Christianity, which would reap memorable harvests in Romanized Africa. Just think of the future works of Saint Augustine.

Even before subduing Carthage, Rome had extended its dominion toward the West and toward the East. To the West, with an action begun in 218 [B.C.], it had acquired the Iberian Peninsula, which became—in 195 [B.C.]—the *provincia Hispania* [province of Spain]. In the East, fighting against the successors of Alexander the Great, it had conquered a large part of what had been Alexander's vast empire. Its victories over the Antigonides, Philip V, and Perseus of Macedonia (at Cynoscephalae in 193 and at Pydna in 168, respectively) had opened up to Rome the roads of Greece; the victory over Antiochus III, a descendant of Seleucus, won in 190 [B.C.] at Magnesia ad Sipylum [on the Sipylus River] in Asia Minor, gave it access to Syria and to the regions of far-off Asia.

A singular destiny willed that the year 146 B.C. would see, along with the destruction of Carthage, that of Corinth as well. The latter marked the end of Greek liberty, which had been defended valiantly by the Achaean league, but at the same time it was also the beginning of the great expansion of Greek culture in Italy.

This was followed, in the next century, by the campaigns of Pompey against Mithridates, king of Pontus, campaigns that in 64 [B.C.] enriched the already immense dominion of Rome with the territories of Pontus and Bithynia; then followed, between the years 57 and 50 [B.C.], the famous expedition of Caesar into Gaul, thanks to which Roman culture reached the Rhine River.

In 31 B.C. another province came to be added to the domain of Rome: the fertile and splendid land of Egypt. This occurred at the conclusion of the civil war that had been afflicting Rome in the preceding years. The decisive battle between the two last rivals, Octavian and Antony, took place in September of the year 31 [B.C.] near the promontory of Actium on the Ionic coast of central Greece, and victory smiled upon Octavian. Antony committed suicide, as did Cleopatra, the last queen of Egypt, who was involved with Antony. Thus it was that Egypt came under Roman rule.

Four years later Octavian solemnly assumed the supreme authority and, together with it, the title of *Augustus*, which, being derived from the verb *augere*, contained within it the idea of "increase", of "prosperity". Here, the Roman Empire was born.

Rome, as a free republic, had managed, thanks to its prodigious development, to extend its dominion over a vast stretch of land and sea that was practically identical with the then-known world. After the founding of the empire, this territory grew still more with the annexation of the regions of the Germanic tribes and the Danube basin. The empire of Augustus extended, in essence, between the Iberian

Peninsula and the course of the Euphrates River, between Germany, with the Danube region, and northern Africa.[7]

This was the impressive reality of the Roman Empire; a reality that certainly prompted reflection. This happened, for example, with Titus Livius, the great historian of Rome. At a certain point in his *History*, he goes back in thought to the past empire of Alexander the Great and asks himself an interesting question: What would have occurred if Alexander, instead of turning toward the East, had turned toward the West? For Livius, the question is resolved in an exaltation of the military might of the ancient Romans, against which the audacity of the young Macedonian king would have been smashed.[8] In reality, it is permissible to say today that Alexander's expedition (and he alone, in those days, could have put it into action) was the necessary prerequisite for the future expansion of the Roman Empire in Asia and, indirectly, for the spread of Christianity.

But let us turn to Augustus and to the empire he founded. Henceforth, over this immense dominion would reign, according to the will of the ruler, a sovereign peace, the bearer of well-being and happiness. This is what Augustus wanted to express when he ordered the splendid *Ara Pacis Augustae* [altar/monument of the Augustan peace] to arise in Rome, on the Field of Mars [*Campo Marzio*]. It was solemnly dedicated on June 30 of the year 9 B.C.

Now, it is perhaps not by sheer chance that after an extremely short interval of time, in Bethlehem, a remote vil-

---

[7] After Augustus, the Roman Empire extended farther to the north. In the second century Trajan conquered Dacia, and his successor, Adrian, brought about, at Vallum Caledoniae, the conquest of Britain, which had been begun by Claudius in the preceding century.

[8] Livius 9, 17–19.

lage of distant Palestine, Jesus Christ was born, whose doctrine was destined to spread under the sign of peace through the entire world.[9]

And, if one reflects a little, the Roman Empire was indeed necessary for the spread of this religion. The universal message of Christ, which preached the brotherhood of all men, as sons of a common heavenly Father, in fact had need—in order to be brought to the knowledge of all—of a universal structure capable of receiving and propagating it. And such a structure could only be the universal empire that had been almost prodigiously created by Rome and of which Rome was the center.

What—we might ask ourselves—did Rome give to Christianity? It gave it, in the first place, the very universality of its empire, with the many roads that the Roman genius had been able to pave on land and the many shipping routes that it had established on the sea, so as to connect to Rome all the places, even the most distant, in the vast world that obeyed it. Then it gave it, as a means and a model, its own perfect organization. We have already seen that at the end of the first century Clement, the head of the Christian community of Rome, pointed out to the Corinthians, who were quarreling among themselves, the example of the Roman legion, which was marvelously well organized.[10] And to this military organization was united the no less admirable juridical and administrative organization to which Christianity not

[9] Jesus was born, as is well known, during a census while Herod was king of Palestine; certainly before the year 4 B.C. (death of Herod) and probably in 8 B.C., the year in which the census decreed by Augustus seems to have been carried out in the Palestine region (cf. S. Accame, in *Rivista di Filologia e d'istruzione classica* 23–24 [1944–1945]: 138–70).

[10] See above, pp. 24–25.

infrequently had occasion to conform itself. Again, the empire offered Christianity an enormous cultural and religious heritage, which, once it came in contact with the new faith and was transfigured by it, sometimes brought about an influential ferment in the spiritual life.

Finally, there is one other important advantage worth noting that Christianity derived from the empire. I mean the use of a language understandable by all, which was capable of spreading the good news as precisely and rapidly as possible among the ever-increasing numbers of Christ's followers. The empire, as you know, was bi-lingual: in the West, Latin prevailed, but in the East, Greek, and the latter had become fixed in that "common" language (*koiné*), which from the fourth century B.C. had replaced the variety of Greek dialects. There were, however, already in the empire of Augustus, many who understood and spoke both languages. Greek, naturally, lent itself better to a doctrine that originated in the East; and in fact the New Testament is composed in *koiné* Greek. But the close relationship between Greek and Latin within the territories of the empire was one reason why the message of Christ came to be known rapidly throughout the empire.

If the Roman Empire gave all this to Christianity, Rome in turn received from Christianity a unique privilege: that of a perennial vitality. Other famous cities of antiquity had died, one after the other, with the empires of which they had been the centers; Rome, on the other hand, remained and remains, thanks precisely to Christianity. In Rome, indeed, the fleeting empire founded by Augustus was succeeded by the perennial empire of the universal, that is "catholic", Church, which by a singular concurrence of events—too singular to be considered anything but providential—Christianity had founded there.

But what was the reason for and, with it, the guarantee of the universality and thus of the perennial vitality of Rome? I believe that I am not mistaken in thinking of the presence, in Rome, of the tomb and of the exceptionally authentic relics of Peter, that is, of the apostle upon whom Christ himself declared that he would found his Church, promising that the powers of evil would not prevail against it.

This is, I believe, the secret whereby Rome, "the predestined city", has resisted and resists the attrition of time and of human errors.

APPENDIX

VIRGIL'S FOURTH *ECLOGUE*

On this subject of the relation between Rome and nascent Christianity, we cannot entirely overlook the fourth *Eclogue* of Virgil. In this poem, indeed, many Christians recognized, at least from the fourth century on, a suggestive omen concerning the birth of Jesus; moreover, from this very poem was derived, in large measure, the reputation that Virgil had during the Middle Ages of being a prophet, or even a wizard [*magus*].

The *Eclogue* was written in Rome, very probably, as we will see, in the year 40 B.C., that is, more than thirty years before Jesus was born in the cave of Bethlehem. This eclogue is different from the other nine that Virgil wrote. The poet himself states this at the beginning of the poem. Whereas in the others he sang of scenes from pastoral life, in this one he proposes to treat a loftier theme (*paulo maiora canamus* [we sing of somewhat greater things]). It is about a consul to whom Virgil, his friend, wishes to pay homage. This high-ranking personage, who is mentioned explicitly in verses 11 and following, is Gaius Asinius Pollio, who held that office in that very year, 40 B.C.

In his verses, Virgil extols a newborn infant, a prodigious creature whose appearance will renew the world and will bring it peace and happiness. There shall be, in short, a new *magnus ordo* ["great order" of the world], which will be initiated precisely with the consulate of Pollio.

The birth of the fortunate child is portrayed by the poet in an exalted vision. The world is one great festival of flowers and perfumes; the golden age returns; justice is restored; above all, peace is reestablished among the creatures of the universe, men and animals. All this the child will bring with him when he descends from heaven's height, as the poet explicitly states (verse 7: *iam nova progenies caelo demittitur alto* [Now the new offspring is sent down from high heaven]).

The boy who comes down from heaven's height and renews the world called to mind, for many early Christians, the verses of the Old Testament in which the prophet Isaiah speaks of the "shoot" that is born "from the stump of Jesse" [Is 11:1] (that is, from the line of David), who will bring with him a universal peace and glory for the people of Israel;[1] and since the "shoot" announced by Isaiah was very soon interpreted by the Christians as Christ, the Redeemer of the world, who established a new order, it was only a short step from there to recognizing Christ in Virgil's *puer* [boy] as well. The Christian interpretation of the fourth *Eclogue*, which was extended also to other hints found in the Bible, appeared, as it seems, for the first time in the writings of Eusebius, bishop of Caesarea, that is, in the first half of the fourth century, and then had, as I said, great success.[2]

In reality, Virgil's *puer* who is about to be born is not Jesus, but rather a Roman baby, very probably (almost all scholars today agree) the future son of that same Gaius Asinius Pollio whom the poet mentions, a child who, to be precise, received the name of Saloninus. It is clear that we are dealing with a simple human creature, both from the repeated mention of the consul (obviously the father), and also from the allusion to the mother, who, after the pains of pregnancy, prepares to receive the newborn with her smile (verses 61ff.). But why, one might

---

[1] Is 11.

[2] Eusebius, *Constantini oratio ad sanctorum coetum* (*Patrologia Graeca*, 20, 129, 2).

ask, did Virgil want to portray a normal human birth in a grandiose scene having a universal character? No doubt, we might
reply, so as to render an exceptional homage to a friend in authority. It is permissible, however, to suppose that this obvious motive was seconded by Virgil's desire to give poetic form
to an idea that was very widespread in that era: the idea, I mean,
of an imminent and universal new beginning that would bring
to suffering humanity the gift of peace and the wellbeing that
follows from it. This idea, which originated in the East, cir-
culated widely in the West also and was promoted there by the
spread of the Sibylline Oracles. It is not too fanciful to think
that, like other people and perhaps more than other people,
Virgil sensed the fascination of this idea, so much so as to derive from it his inspiration while singing the future birth awaited
by his friend, the consul.

But at this point another consideration joins the preceding circumstances. In October of the year 40 [B.C.] a peace
treaty was concluded at Brindisi between Octavian and Antony, which was to end a lamentable period of rivalry and
distress; and the mediator of the agreement was, together
with Maecenas, none other than Gaius Asinius Pollio, a friend
of Antony. Certainly it is not impossible that the atmosphere
of relief and of hope resulting from that peace played some
part in the poetic creation of the fourth *Eclogue*.

However, together with the widespread conviction that a
happy and universal new beginning was near, it is possible
that another influence on Virgil's thought may have been a
direct knowledge of the Hebrew tradition relative to the coming of the Messiah. Some scholars maintain this, recalling
appropriately that Asinius Pollio had ties of close friendship
with the king of Judaea, Herod the Great.[3] Then, too, in

[3] Cf. Flavius Josephus, *Antiquitates Iudicae* 15, 343.

that very autumn of 40 B.C. Herod traveled to Rome seeking help against the Parthians.[4] Besides, even if we disregard the friendship between Asinius Pollio and Herod and the latter's visit to Rome in the year 40, it cannot be overlooked that a flourishing colony of Jews lived in Rome at that time, as the chronology of the Jewish catacombs in the Trastevere district demonstrates. Thus Virgil might have learned in other ways, too, about the long-awaited Messiah of the Jews.

Examining Virgil's *Eclogue* attentively, at the place that describes the idyllic picture of the world at peace, we notice that the poet follows not so much the biblical text from Isaiah as the classic description of the Isles of the Blessed, such as Horace presents, for example, in his sixteenth *Epode*.[5] Note, too, that this poem was written in 41 B.C., just one year before the probable date of the Virgilian *Eclogue*, when Horace, afflicted by the scourge of the civil wars, sought refuge and consolation in the ideal vision of the delightful Isles. The Horatian poem, however, lacks the characteristic mention of the child who is about to be born, which appears, on the other hand, as an essential element both in the *Eclogue* and in the Hebrew text.

At any rate, it is a suggestive thought that, when the birth of Christ was imminent, a voice—of a great poet—was lifted up at Rome, of all places, which albeit indirectly and unconsciously leads us back to the central event of history: the appearance on earth of the long-awaited Messiah.[6]

---

[4] Ibid., 14, 487.

[5] Horace, *Epod.* 16, vv. 41–64.

[6] The "mysterious" fourth *Eclogue* has occasioned a vast number of literary works, in some of which fantasy plays more than a small role. Anyone who wants some idea of the enormous bibliography pertaining to this poem should see M. Schaur and C. Hosius, *Geschichte der römischen Literatur*, vol. 2 (Munich, 1935), pp. 42–46; A. Ceresa-Gastaldo, in *Enciclopedia Virgiliana*, vol. 1 (Rome, 1984), pp. 936f.

CONCLUSIONS AND FINAL REFLECTIONS

The spiritual primacy of the Church of Rome was very soon recognized, without reservations, by the Christian generations that followed the advent of Christianity. Certain non-Catholic scholars have tried to attribute this recognition solely to the circumstance that Rome was at that time the capital of the empire. In reality, this reason, which is a bit simplistic, is joined by other more profound ones, which in the second century were set forth by Irenaeus, bishop of Lyons. Be that as it may, it is certain that very important factors in the recognition of that primacy were: the immediate and undeniable proof of the universality of the Church of Rome (a universality that was no less evident than that of the empire), and also the certainty that Rome had witnessed the preaching of *both* apostles who had suffered martyrdom and had been buried in that very city of Rome. Most remarkable of all, though, for the recognition of the primacy, was the presence in Rome of the tomb of Peter, that is, of the apostle upon whom Christ himself had declared that he would build his Church.

Around the middle of the third century a factor opposed to the recognition of the primacy began to appear in the Church of Rome: the transfer of the supreme authority of the Church (in the collective sense of a religious entity) to the sole person of the bishop [of Rome]. Another negative element was added in 756 with the acquisition of the temporal authority. Then followed in 1054 the separation of the Church of Constantinople from Rome, a separation that disrupted the unity of the Church and thereby necessarily detracted from the primacy of Rome. In the West, however, this primacy remained strong in practice until the end of the Middle Ages.

The sixteenth century saw the inauspicious attack on the Church of Rome by the Reformation (Luther, the Anglicans, Calvin); but, on the other hand, the Counter-Reformation, the Council of Trent, and the splendid victory over the Turks at Lepanto were events that greatly heightened the prestige of the Roman Church.

In the seventeenth century, the damage of the so-called wars of religion between Protestants and Catholics was partially compensated for by the new and decisive victory of the Catholics over the Turks at Vienna.

In the eighteenth and nineteenth centuries the Roman Church was sorely tried by the Enlightenment movement, by the French Revolution, by the events of the Napoleonic era, and by the liberal movement.

We have to proceed to the twentieth century in order to witness a great increase in the prestige of the Roman Church. First the *Conciliazione* with Italy (1929), by liberating the Church almost completely from that temporal power which for centuries had encumbered her, restored to her the full freedom to expand spiritually; then Pius XII, with his personal authority and with his enlightened and untiring work, won for her the respect of the whole world.

After so many centuries, and notwithstanding many adverse circumstances and not a few errors, which can be blamed partly on the customs of the times, partly on human weakness, the Church of Rome remains, today, alive and vital.

Assurance and proof of her exceptional vitality and of her legitimate spiritual primacy are certain persistent "primacies" that she alone retains and by which she undeniably distinguishes herself from the other Christian Churches. She indeed, and only she, still possesses today, by a singular privilege, the oldest Christian basilica, the oldest portrait of Christ, the oldest portrait of the Blessed Virgin, the oldest Christian statue, and oldest scientifically proven Christian relic that is known thus far anywhere in the world: the bones of Peter in the Vatican basilica.

Of all the "primacies" the last-mentioned is the most important, and also, we must admit, the most impressive. It is in fact a great thing for the Catholic Church that the mortal remains of Peter still exist in the Vatican basilica. These go back to the first century, that is, to the origins of the Church of Rome and of Christianity in general. And it is no mere coincidence that those relics, almost miraculously preserved, belong to an apostle who not only knew Christ personally and was a witness to his miracles, but was chosen by Christ himself to be the foundation of his Church and thus the depositary of his doctrine and his successor on earth.

The existence and the authenticity of the relics of Peter are (it will not be inappropriate to repeat it once again) scientifically proved by the marvelous convergence of findings provided by various academic disciplines (history, archaeology, topography, epigraphy, numismatics), findings to which are added, by way of confirmation, those of various experimental sciences (anthropology, chemistry, petrography, the technology of commerce).

In short, the Catholic (that is, "universal") Church, which has as her center Rome and, more precisely, the tomb of Peter in the Vatican, is truly the one founded by Christ. Precisely this was the thought expressed many times, with brilliant intuition, by Pius XII, even before the final

conclusion of the investigations beneath the Vatican basilica (the identification of the bones of Peter) had been
reached.[1]

The fact that the universal Catholic Church is the very
one founded by Christ and that her center is the tomb of
Peter in the Vatican basilica is confirmed, finally, by a sur-
vey of the records concerning the historical events that
preceded, accompanied, and would immediately follow
the formation of the Roman Empire, which was the admirable structure necessary for the spread of Christianity, while
Christianity gave to Rome, the custodian of the tomb of
Peter, a unique privilege: lasting universality and perennial
vitality.

And now I come to the reflections.

Nowadays there is much talk, in ecclesiastical circles, of
"ecumenism". As in so many other words, the Greek suffix
-ism (ισμός) signifies a theoretical vision. In our case, then,
the theoretical vision is broadened to include all "inhabited
territory" (οἰκουμενη), that is, the whole world.

As applied to Christianity, the term denotes the trend
that seeks, in a spirit of fraternity, the common spiritual
and supernatural values that exist in the various Christian
denominations and thereby to bind more closely the existing ties among the various Churches that acknowledge Christ
to be the divine Master. The ecumenical trend was manifested more decisively, and with a wider vision, after the
Second Vatican Council (1962–1965). From a concern with
the Christian denominations, ecumenism has in fact broadened its interests to encompass all religions, for the purpose

[1] Cf. in particular, *Discorsi e radiomessaggi di S.S. Pio XII*, vol. 1 (Milan,
1961), p. 391.

of appreciating the spiritual principles that are present in each one of them.[2]

In a word, according to this new understanding of the term, all the religions in the world are placed in close contact with one another, thanks precisely to those more or less evident spiritual elements that each one of them contains.

In this very broad ecumenical movement the Catholic Church of Rome, beginning with the pontificate of John XXIII and down to that of John Paul II, has certainly not been absent. On the contrary, she has taken part in it many times and, what is more important, has done so at the official initiatives of her pontiffs, initiatives that are usually accompanied by rather eloquent gestures.

Those initiatives and those gestures are too well known for us to have to recall them here in detail. We might ask ourselves instead what thoughts they have provoked in those who are Catholic but who, in that very capacity, want to adhere faithfully to the norms of truth.

First of all we need to recognize that those initiatives and those gestures were surely inspired by a good intention: that of establishing an ever more far-reaching understanding among the peoples who dwell on this planet of ours.

But if it is our duty to recognize this good intention, it is no less a duty to point out that the above-mentioned initiatives and the above-mentioned gestures, upon which the highest authority of the respective participants confers a remarkable importance, are such as to produce doubts and disorientation in the souls of the faithful and thereby run the risk of being dangerous to a greater or lesser extent, and hence

[2] For the meaning of the term "ecumenism" and its evolution, cf. N. Zingarelli, *Il Nuovo Zingarelli: Vocabolario della lingua italiana*, 11th ed. (Bologna, 1987), p. 626.

contrary to the interests of the Church that—in their intentions—they should be serving.

Let it be noted immediately that it makes a certain impression when one sees Christianity, if not confused with non-Christian religions, at least lined up with them. I do not think that I am expressing a new idea in declaring that Christ brought into the world a doctrine that is not interchangeable, which cannot be compared, even remotely, with other religious doctrines, whether they be older or more recent. Gaetano de Sanctis, to whom these pages of mine are dedicated, a profound connoisseur of antiquity and of early Christianity, used to declare that he was more and more amazed, the more he studied the revolution that Christ had brought about in the society of that time; so much so that he felt more and more reaffirmed in the conviction that Christianity had divine origins.

In our case, if we wish to consider the two principal non-Christian religions to which the new ecumenism is being extended, that is, the monotheistic religions of the Jews and of the Muslims, several obvious reflections are inevitable.

As for the Jews, everyone knows that, far from recognizing in Jesus of Nazareth the divine and long-desired Messiah, they are still awaiting the fulfillment of the promise handed down by the biblical prophets.

Then, as to the Muslims, who appeared in history with the seventh century A.D. (Muhammad, their founder, died in 632), I would like to say a few more words about them. There are radical contrasts between their religion and Christianity. While not entirely denying Christ, the Muslims completely refuse to recognize his divinity and consider him a mere prophet, whereas Muhammad, who concludes the series of prophets, is for them the prophet par excellence of the most-high God, Allah. Note, furthermore, that the most sacred object in Islamic worship is the famous "black rock", venerated in Mecca in the Ka'ba, a little cubic building. This rock had been adored in the pre-Islamic period and then it was promoted by Muhammad to the dignity of a heavenly symbol. There is more. A profound abyss separates the concept of Islamic paradise from that of Christian paradise. Whereas, indeed, for Christians paradise consists of a supreme spiritual happiness, that of the full and direct vision of God, the paradise of the Muslims assumes a character of material and almost sensual concreteness. It is imagined as an immense garden, with plentiful shade, with perfumed watercourses and rivers of milk and honey, a bower in which delicious fruits hang from the trees.[3] Besides satisfying their hunger and quenching their thirst, the happy inhabitants of the garden enjoy the presence of extremely beautiful women with luminous dark-brown eyes (the *houri*), who serve as their companions. Surely, there could be no more jarring contrast between this concept and that of the Christian family based upon monogamous, indissoluble marriage, which in turn serves as the basis for human society.

Moving along, then, from the non-Christian religions of the Jews and the Muslims to the other, Christian denominations that the new ecumenism tries to embrace (Orthodox, Lutheran, Anglican, Calvinist), I can only refer to what I have already written about them; which made it clear that they are far from being able to compete with the two-thousand-year tradition of the Catholic Church, founded in Rome upon the tomb of Peter. Besides, this very tomb, which

[3] An immense, shady, and well-watered garden lends itself to being the dream of someone who lives in the desert landscape of Arabia. It could also be that the refreshing garden of Muslim paradise goes back to some extent to the memory of the patterned images in Syriac mosaics.

is the strength and the supreme guarantee of the Catholic Church, is also the reef against which the claims of the other Churches are dashed, as we have seen.

It is necessary to add that the ecumenism of which I have spoken thus far, that is, the ecumenism that is carried on with the right intention, has lent itself and lends itself to harmful intrusions of that false ecumenism which is influenced by forces that operate in the shadows and aims to acquire, not spiritual benefits, but the temporal and material goods of this world and tends above all to satisfy the thirst for power. Let anyone who wants to understand, understand.

These are, if I am not mistaken, the dangers that may be encountered by the gestures, however sincere, that are dictated by the new ecumenism.

Well, then, what is to be done?

Nowadays there is a common perception that the world is heading toward unity. Therefore Christ's precept becomes more and more relevant: the most important precept, which commands us to love all men as sons of the same heavenly Father, not only our friends but also our enemies.

The final commandment given by Christ to the apostles was to bring the good news to all men, so that there might be one fold and one shepherd.[4] The apostles obeyed this command and are still obeying it today. This is demonstrated by the missionaries who, braving hardships and dangers and sometimes death as well, travel the paths of the world even to the farthest lands in order to spread wherever possible the teaching of Christ. Such great efforts, such heroic sacrifices tend, however, to attract souls so as to lead them into the

---

[4] Jn 10:16.

one true Church, that is, into the universal Church that has her center in Rome over the tomb of Peter.

True ecumenism demands (no doubt) that we consider all men, according to the Gospel standard, to be brothers and that we love and help them as such. But in doing this we are not allowed to forget which is the true universal Church, guaranteed by clear providential signs. To forget this would be tantamount to trampling upon history and denying the truth.

On September 10, 1990, the present pope, John Paul II, during his seventh pastoral visit to Africa, consecrated at Yamoussoukro, in the Ivory Coast, a magnificent church dedicated to Our Lady of Peace and conformed to the image and likeness of the Basilica of Saint Peter in the Vatican (figure 12).

In 1986 the president of that far-off country, Felix Houphouët Boigny, at the age of eighty, had begun to realize the most ambitious dream of his life: that of erecting the largest Catholic basilica in all Africa, which could become the meeting place for all the Catholics on that continent. The construction, which was entrusted to an architect of Lebanese extraction, Pierre Fakkoury, was executed very rapidly and was completed in 1989.

Built upon a large estate donated by the same president, the edifice has dimensions even larger than those of its imposing Roman model and also has at its disposal an adjoining episcopal palace and a residence suitable for hosting the pope on those occasions when he is staying on African soil. Vast gardens surround it on all sides.

It is not difficult to imagine how much labor and how much expense the work required. The figures would make your head spin. This provoked various critical remarks. How could anyone condone channeling that enormous flow of money to such an undertaking, in a land that is beset by urgent economic problems? How could anyone justify the existence of a spectacular church building side by side with miserable huts inhabited by people who are deprived of basic conveniences?

In the homily he gave during the consecration of the church,[5] the pope sought to respond to these criticisms, calling to mind that on every continent the children of God have dedicated the best of their art to the building destined to be the house in which God himself dwells in their midst. In a word, it is a question of an act of love that finds in itself its justification. In reality, this is true. It is also appropriate to recall, in this connection, the well-known Gospel episode in which Jesus, a guest at the house in Bethany, justifies as an act of love the deed of Mary, the sister of Lazarus, who anointed his feet with costly perfumes and dried them with her hair, as opposed to the criticism of Judas, who claimed that that ointment could have been sold for the benefit of the poor.[6]

In his homily, the pope touches also upon other arguments besides the one that I have mentioned. Thus he exalts the Blessed Virgin, the patroness of peace, to whom the new edifice is dedicated, and he associates her with Christ the Savior, hoping that many believers will gather here, within these walls, in the joy of the eucharistic feast.

There is, however, one thought that, strangely enough, does not appear in the homily of the pontiff, a thought that nevertheless, it seems to me, is illuminating and comforting.

---

[5] Reproduced in *L'Osservatore Romano* [Italian edition], September 10–11, 1990, p. 10.

[6] Jn 12:3–8. In Judas' remark there is also the hypocrisy of someone who, greedily, would have liked to appropriate that money.

The new and magnificent edifice, with which (these are the pope's words) the Church has become more deeply implanted in the African soil, reproduces, in even greater proportions, the Basilica of Saint Peter in the Vatican. Why the Basilica of Saint Peter? Clearly, because the Catholics of Africa have felt that only the Basilica of Saint Peter, the center of the Church, was capable of expressing fully the religious ideal of their souls. Of course, beneath the enormous dome of the new building you do not find the precious object around which—in Rome—both the Michelangelesque cupola and all the rest of the basilica, as well as, spiritually, the entire Catholic Church, gravitate: I mean the mortal remains of the Prince of the Apostles. But the image of the true Roman basilica it is, and it keeps alive in the minds of the faithful of that far-off land the thought that precisely the Vatican basilica of Rome, with its unique and priceless relic, is the center of the universal Church, to which they fervently adhere.

The new basilica, so laboriously constructed in the Ivory Coast, at the edge of the desert, is—it seems to me—not only an act of love for God, but also a profession of faith in the Roman Church and, together with that, an acknowledgment of her spiritual primacy.

The thought suggested by the recent consecration of the church in the Ivory Coast suggests in turn another one, with which I would like to conclude these pages of mine.

Even more recently, on the occasion of Easter, the present pontiff, John Paul II, speaking from the central balcony of the Vatican basilica, addressed *Urbi et Orbi* [to the city and to the world] the traditional message and imparted to the whole world, in fifty-eight languages, the traditional apostolic blessing. In this circumstance, too, he did not mention Peter; yet he made an implicit reference to him, declaring that he was speaking to the world from "the heart of the Church". What, indeed, is the "heart of the Church", if not the Basilica of Saint Peter in the Vatican?

To speak to the world is the legitimate prerogative of the head of that Church which calls herself Catholic, that is, "universal"; a prerogative clearly confirmed by the exceptional presence in Rome, and specifically in the Vatican basilica, of the authentic tomb of Peter and of his authentic relics. The ancient universality of Rome, the predestined city, is prolonged in time with the spiritual universality of the "one, holy, catholic, and apostolic" Church, as the faithful for centuries have professed her to be.

From such a Church, and only from her, can the voice of the pontiff truly address all of humanity.

INDEX